THE SELF-ESTEEM (CBT) WORKBOOK FOR ADULTS

A Cognitive Behavior Therapy and Positive Psychology Guide to Move Past Self-Doubt, Quiet the Inner Critic, and Improve Confidence

MARCEE A. MARTIN

Contents

The Epidemic of Low Self-Esteem	1
CHAPTER 1 *Loving Yourself Unconditionally*	11
What Is Self-Esteem?	11
What Is Self-Acceptance?	21
What Is Self-Love?	27
How Do They All Relate?	30
CHAPTER 2 *The Roots of Self-Doubt*	32
CHAPTER 3 *A Cognitive Behavioral Therapy Approach to Self-Doubt*	44
Understanding Cognitive Behavioral Therapy	44
Cognitive Behavioral Therapy Exercises	49
CHAPTER 4 *The Power of Positive Psychology*	57
Understanding Self-Worth	58
Positive Psychology Exercises	65
CHAPTER 5 *Perfectionism No More*	73
Understanding Perfectionism	73
Exercises to Reduce Your Perfectionism	77
CHAPTER 6 *Venturing Into the Past for Big Rewards*	82
Understanding Shame	83
How to Explore Your Past	87
CHAPTER 7 *Using Radical Compassion to Silence Your Inner Critic*	93
Radical Compassion Exercises	95

CHAPTER 8 — 100
Positive Psychology Exercises, CBT Worksheets, and Life-Changing Self-Doubt Quotes

Positive Psychology Exercises — 100

CBT Worksheets — 103

Self-Doubt Quotes — 107

Taking Control of Your Own Life — 110

References — 117

© **Copyright 2022 - All rights reserved.**

The content contained within this book may not be reproduced, duplicated or transmitted without direct written permission from the author or the publisher.

Under no circumstances will any blame or legal responsibility be held against the publisher, or author, for any damages, reparation, or monetary loss due to the information contained within this book, either directly or indirectly.

Legal Notice:

This book is copyright protected. It is only for personal use. You cannot amend, distribute, sell, use, quote or paraphrase any part, or the content within this book, without the consent of the author or publisher.

Disclaimer Notice:

Please note the information contained within this document is for educational and entertainment purposes only. All effort has been executed to present accurate, up to date, reliable, complete information. No warranties of any kind are declared or implied. Readers acknowledge that the author is not engaged in the rendering of legal, financial, medical or professional advice. The content within this book has been derived from various sources. Please consult a licensed professional before attempting any techniques outlined in this book.

By reading this document, the reader agrees that under no circumstances is the author responsible for any losses, direct or indirect, that are incurred as a result of the use of the information contained within this document, including, but not limited to, errors, omissions, or inaccuracies.

$129 FREE

Achieve a Worry-Free Smile with these
12 Mental Health Books!

The Easy Way to Improve Mental Health

Therapy doesn't have to be so expensive and complicated. That's why we are giving you these 7 eBooks and 5 bonus workbooks so you can start improving your mental health right away, without leaving your home!

- **Stop Worrying All the Time**: Stop those nagging thoughts in their tracks with mindfulness and anti-anxiety tips expert CBT therapists use!
- **Do Therapy Your Way**: Start taking action with 5 BONUS workbooks, so you can start smiling, laughing, and enjoying life on your own!
- **Love Yourself, Love Others**: Enhance your career, relationships, hobbies, and more as you march through each day with confident self-esteem

Scan to download:

Loved this book? You may also want the other books in this series:

What others are saying:

Christina Forster

★★★★★ **Great book!**
Reviewed in the United States on January 31, 2023
Verified Purchase

This book is so helpful in learning about self-worth and self-esteem and different treatments to help. It was interesting reading about how self-doubt can creep in and start to cause a decrease in self-esteem and self-confidence. Certain things such as perfectionism can lead to self-doubt. I enjoyed learning more about CBT and how to use it to help with one's sense of self. CBT can help you overcome self-doubt. It is explained in a very easy to understand way. I really enjoyed the chapter on radical self-compassion. If we could all learn to be kinder to ourselves it would go a long way!

A D

★★★★★ **Improve your confidence**
Reviewed in the United States on January 30, 2023
Verified Purchase

If you are your own worst critic like me then this book can help. They provide positive psychology exercises and CBT worksheets to help you overcome your mind and silence your inner critics. You learn ways to reduce perfectionism. Explain the roots of self-doubt and provide exercises to work on understanding yourself worth. I love chapter 7 that gives exercises for radical compassion. By the end I gained useful tools to help me take more control of my life.

Daniela Hernández

★★★★★ **Healing book**
Reviewed in the United States on January 30, 2023
Verified Purchase

Unfortunately a few years ago I had a relationship that lowered my self-esteem and now I'm trying to start a new relationship with another person. However, my lack of self-esteem is affecting both of us. This book helped me heal many wounds and love myself over anything else.

Scan to check out books on Amazon →

To My Faithful Readers,

This book is dedicated to you, my amazing readers! Thank you for accompanying me on this journey. I hope that you will find the information in this book helpful in improving your self-esteem. I would like to remind you that the best way to improve your self-esteem is to practice the exercises in this workbook regularly. Remember, you are not alone in this struggle. With determination, time, and patience, you can overcome your self-doubts and build a more confident version of yourself. I believe in you! Thank you for your support, and I wish you all the best in your journey!

With Love and Pizza,
Marcee

The Epidemic of Low Self-Esteem

Low self-esteem comes from a faulty way of thinking where you view yourself as inadequate, unlovable, or incompetent. Once you develop low self-esteem, this thinking error can permeate your every thought and action, resulting in erroneous assumptions and ongoing self-defeating behavior. Low self-esteem is a common occurrence, and most people will have experienced it at some point in their life. Others who are more affected by low self-esteem may struggle with it for years as their characters revolve around this trait. When you have low self-esteem, this may also lead you to have low self-confidence, low self-value, and poor relationships with others. You may also develop maladaptive coping methods in an attempt to deal with your low self-esteem, which in turn may lead to various other psychological problems. As you can see, having low self-esteem is a complex problem. Your self-esteem can be affected and caused by several factors, just as it can influence and impact several areas of your life. There are many interplaying and intersecting things to consider when tackling your low self-esteem.

With so many factors to consider, this book aims to lead and guide you through your journey of improving your self-esteem. Wanting to learn how to improve your self-esteem is a common and basic desire. In this sense, it's a simple issue. You're working on the fundamental need to like yourself. On the other hand, when you get down to the nitty-gritty details of it, raising your self-esteem isn't as simple as it may sound. You will need a lot of knowledge, patience, and self-kindness to effectively address this issue. So, this book will consolidate both approaches to raising your self-esteem: It will use simple and accessible language to clearly explain the various intricate details and knowledge that will help you improve your self-esteem. You will be taught in-depth knowledge in a way that is easily understandable.

Before you learn more about this book, let's explore more about you—the reader. This book is aimed at any reader who wishes to unlock their highest potential, achieve their deepest desires, and delve into the world of being self-confident. If your self-esteem has been an issue for you for a while, but you've been unsure how to address it, this book is for you. Several of your needs may be met through the content of these pages: Your need for a cognitive behavioral therapy (CBT) guide for self-esteem that teaches you how to use CBT to build and maintain healthy self-esteem and have a better sense of self-worth; Your need for a positive psychology book that teaches you the components of self-love and radical compassion, and helps you put an end to your perfectionist mindset; and your need for a self-doubt workbook that contains activities and exercises that will help you build more confidence in yourself.

By meeting these needs, you will hopefully be able to address some of the problems and pains that you've been experiencing in your life. Maybe your low self-esteem has been affecting your interpersonal relationships and making you anxious all the time. When your self-esteem is low, your relationships may suffer as you may develop a doormat personality, you may never stand up for yourself, and you may accept whatever treatment you get (no matter how horrible). You may even become more anxious as you don't believe in your own abilities to overcome any hardships (no matter how big or small). Maybe you have a mindset that constantly tells you that you're not good or perfect enough, thus preventing you from doing certain things for fear of failure or imperfection. Having low self-esteem can be extremely limiting as you become intensely afraid of failure. You may believe that anything less than perfection is a negative comment on yourself as a person, so you may become fearful of trying new things or trying at all. Or maybe you exhibit self-doubt and low self-confidence to such an extreme that you sabotage yourself, making those around you lack confidence in your skills and abilities and enforcing your lack of trust in yourself. As previously mentioned, self-esteem relates to self-confidence and self-doubt, so that these traits may be exacerbated by your low self-esteem. Once heightened, they can lead to several other maladaptive behaviors, such as self-sabotage. If these issues relate to you, then you can be sure that you will benefit from this book.

Despite facing a myriad of nuanced issues (all coming from your low self-esteem), there is a solution to your ails. This book represents a detailed guide that will give you step-by-step instructions on how to create and maintain your sense of self-worth and self-esteem. CBT is a renowned and recognized form of therapy that has proven effective in building and maintaining healthy self-esteem. This treatment method can even help you change your negative habits and replace them with more effective strategies. In this book, you will learn several CBT exercises to help you achieve these goals. You will also learn about positive psychology, which will be effective in helping you overcome your perfectionist mindset. A perfectionist mindset can set you up for failure and unhappiness in various ways. By discarding this mindset, you can remove the handicap you've placed on yourself and make room for better ways of thinking. For example, positive psychology will encourage you to have more compassion for yourself by teaching you about self-love. Self-love is an important component of self-improvement, and it will be a significant help to you as you strive to improve your self-esteem. Finally, you will be able to address your self-doubt and self-confidence by reading this book. You will be led through interesting activities and exercises that can increase your confidence and trust in your own abilities.

Now that you're more familiar with who this book is intended for and what benefits you stand to gain from it, let's return to learning about the book, specifically the structure. Understanding how the content is arranged can help you prepare yourself for what information to expect, thus improving your retention and receptiveness. This book is divided into three parts. The first part outlines the relationship between self-esteem, self-love, and self-acceptance and the common causes of low self-esteem. The second part expressly discusses how to use CBT and positive psychology to overcome self-doubt, practice meditation, and develop self-worth. You will also explore how the past may affect your current self-esteem. The third and final part of the book covers the teachings of radical compassion. You will guide your inner voice to be kinder and more understanding. You will even learn how to use positive psychology exercises, self-doubt quotes, and CBT exercises to maintain healthy self-esteem. Overall, you will understand why self-love and self-care practices are crucial in boosting self-esteem, the relationship between self-esteem, self-love, and self-acceptance, and the top and most common causes of low self-esteem. Other aspects include the best principles to deal with self-doubt, everything you need to know about positive psychology and how it helps with self-worth, mistakes to avoid, and how to use CBT to recover from low self-esteem and low self-worth. Finally, the book will show you how radical compassion can silence your inner critic, CBT worksheets and practical exercises to build and maintain healthy self-esteem, how the past affects you and how to rewrite it, and a whole lot more!

To help you really plan out what you will learn from this book and anticipate what content to expect, here is a more thorough and specific breakdown of each chapter. Part 1: An Introduction to Low Self-Esteem consists of Chapters 1 and 2. Chapter 1 focuses on the relationship between self-love, self-acceptance, and self-esteem. Chapter 2 explores the common thieves of self-esteem. These are the prevalent factors that may lead to or contribute to low self-esteem. Part 2: A Step-by-Step Guide to Proven Therapies includes Chapters 3, 4, 5, and 6. Chapter 3 will introduce you to CBT and focus on how you can use its methods and strategies to overcome your issues of self-doubt. Chapter 4 will delve into the power of positive psychology and teach you how you can use its principles to build more self-worth. Chapter 5 will tackle perfectionism and lead you to let go of your perfectionist behaviors, habits, and mindsets. Chapter 6 will venture into your past to improve your present. You will learn how to rewrite your memories from a negative past. Finally, Part 3: Radical Compassion with Practical Exercises consists of Chapters 7 and 8. Chapter 7 addresses the common issue of a harsh and overly critical inner voice. Through radical compassion, you will learn to silence this voice and rewire it to be kinder. Chapter 8 will provide you with worksheets and exercises to aid you along the way as you go forth and continue practicing how to improve and maintain your self-esteem. This chapter will prevent you from backsliding into low self-esteem after you've finished reading this book.

So far, you've received an overview of the type of reader this book is targeted at and a thorough introduction to the content of this book. Now, here's a small introduction to the author. My name is Marcee A. Martin, and I often call myself the happiest author on earth. And this isn't hyperbolic. When I look at my life and reflect, my thoughts are almost always positive. However, my journey to inner happiness was long, protracted, often complex, but fulfilling in the end. In my early teen years, the seeds of low self-esteem, chronic anxiety, non-existent self-confidence, and a plethora of other emotional disorders took root and quickly grew. Before long, I was trapped in an emotional whirlpool that affected my thoughts, actions, and quality of life. I would often confine myself to my room, racked with self-doubt, low energy, negative thoughts, and feelings of inadequacy. This condition continued well into my early twenties. It was then that I noticed just how bad things had gotten. I took a good, long look at myself and my life and realized that my thoughts (particularly those related to my low self-esteem) were negatively affecting every part of my life. Romantically, all my relationships seemed to have ended in much the same way—in a cloud of emotional imbalance, suspicion, toxicity, and unmatched energy. Socially, I had begun to dread every gathering, party, or meet-up—every party and office meeting brought out the worst of my inner demons. Professionally, I wasn't advancing myself as I thought I should have because I wasn't taking hold of any opportunities—I had ideas and contributions to make, but I couldn't vocalize or actualize them out of fear. Personally, I realized that I had grown to hate the sound of my own voice in the presence of other people, and I felt like I always managed to say the wrong things.

This was how I lived my life for years upon years. However, in my late twenties, I finally became conscious and tired of the emotional whirlpool I had been trapped in since my early teen years. I had had enough and was on the brink of a total mental and emotional breakdown, so I decided to start a quest in search of true happiness and emotional balance. I was fired up, motivated, and determined to improve my self-esteem and happiness. That first year, I read over 100 books (across several niches) and watched more than 200 videos on self-improvement. Eventually, the secrets of human relationships and psychology that I unearthed transformed my life. The principles and knowledge that I learned helped me rebuild my relationship with myself, learn self-love, and improve my communication skills with other people. After that long journey, I finally made it out of the emotional darkness that I was in. Now, for the last five years, my new quest has been bringing other people closer to happiness through my books. The pillars of my teachings revolve around: Mindfulness and meditation techniques for anxiety, depression, and stress; The importance of listening (and not just hearing); Ways to challenge and fix cognitive distortions; The best ways to communicate even during difficult times; New methods to shape and discuss with your inner critic; CBT techniques for restoring emotional balance; The importance of self-love, self-esteem, and self-confidence; How to deepen empathetic traits without becoming codependent; How to build conversational skills; Learning to develop charisma and using witty banter to great effect; and Body language clues and how to read between the lines. Obviously, not all these pillars will be used in this book, but they are the common threads that tie together all my books.

I have an ardent passion for helping people overcome issues with their personal perceptions and self-belief, particularly those pertaining to self-esteem problems. Because I relate so deeply to such matters, I am all the more determined to help those going through similar experiences. And the help I offer isn't superficial either. I believe that I have valuable information to share as I've been studying the best methods for getting over the rut of low self-esteem and avoiding self-loathing for at least five years now. Helping you achieve freedom from your negative perceptions about yourself matters deeply to me because what you're about to learn helped me overcome my own struggles and become better at accepting and appreciating my strengths and weaknesses. I understand how difficult it might seem to be starting on the long, arduous journey of overcoming your low self-esteem, and as such, I can show you how to work things out without stress. I'm confident that the strategies I share with you will help you immensely as I have had practical experience with these issues in the past. I was able to find my way out of chronic low self-esteem through CBT and positive psychology methods and practices that you will soon learn. All the mistakes I made in my journey have shaped my expertise in the field, and now I will use those experiences to better guide you so that you don't have to make the same mistakes I did.

I promise you that this book can help you understand the basics and the must-knows about improving your self-esteem that are practical and applicable to you. And after you read this book, you will even be able to begin handling social situations better. It's crucial for you to start understanding how CBT and positive psychology can help you so that you've never caught unawares by your low self-esteem again. So, start your learning right away, and the next time you come face-to-face with low self-esteem or high self-doubt, you'll know exactly what to do. Without further delay, let's start learning how to build and maintain healthy self-esteem. I hope you enjoy the book.

Chapter One

LOVING YOURSELF UNCONDITIONALLY

A fundamental necessity for having high self-esteem is the ability to love yourself unconditionally. This sounds like a simple construct, but in actuality, it's a complex goal to achieve, and it brings in several other traits. Namely, you will need to focus not only on your self-esteem but also on your self-love and self-acceptance. This chapter will start you properly on your journey to building up your self-esteem by going to the root of the issue. You will examine the relationship between your self-esteem, self-love, and self-acceptance. The goal of this chapter is to show you how inseparable these three traits are and how it's important to pay attention to what each of them has to offer in the fight against your low self-esteem. So, you will explore what each of these concepts means individually and then discover how they all connect.

WHAT IS SELF-ESTEEM?

Let's start with the main focus, which is your self-esteem. Everyone knows that having healthy self-esteem is a good and desirable thing. When you have healthy self-esteem, your motivation, mental well-being, happiness, and overall quality of life will be affected and improved. However, it's not a simple thing to have healthy self-esteem. Most people fall into the trap of having self-esteem that is either too high or too low. Both these extremes can be problematic. So it's important to understand where your particular level of self-esteem lies so that you can strike a better balance for yourself. Knowing this will then help you guide yourself better toward achieving healthy self-esteem.

So let's cover the very basics of self-esteem first. What exactly is self-esteem? This trait refers to your overall sense of your own value or worth. It's a measure of how much you value, appreciate, prize, approve of, or like yourself. All this will affect how you treat yourself and your attitude toward yourself. You can understand it in terms of having a favorable or unfavorable attitude toward yourself. Healthy self-esteem allows you to have a healthily favorable attitude toward yourself; low self-esteem causes you to have an unhealthily unfavorable attitude toward yourself, and excessive self-esteem may lead you to have an unhealthily favorable attitude toward yourself. It can be confusing to hear that there can be unhealthy levels of self-esteem or favor. Try to think of it like this. Have you ever witnessed or experienced a referee that was too in favor of a certain player during a sports game? That referee probably treated others unfairly and in a hostile manner while excusing any and all wrongs done by that one player or team. This type of attitude can be very dangerous. In terms of excessive self-esteem, you are the biased and unjust referee, and the player you're favoring is yourself. When this happens, there are several undesirable character traits, behaviors, thoughts, and habits that may arise. For example, you may never think that you're in the wrong, or you may overestimate how skilled you are at something. But more on this topic later on. For now, let's return to defining what self-esteem is.

Another way of understanding this can be that self-esteem is how you value and perceive yourself. Your self-esteem is constructed by your opinions and beliefs about yourself, so it's largely based on your self-perception. This can be problematic as your self-perception is, at once, very volatile and difficult to change. How you view yourself can be volatile as you may see yourself positively or negatively from case to case based on your performance. If you perform well this one time, your self-esteem may receive a momentary boost. But if you mess up for reasons either within or outside your control, your self-esteem may plummet drastically for a while. In this sense, your self-esteem is constantly in flux. Little instances here and there can affect how you view yourself. On the other hand, your opinions and beliefs about yourself can be difficult to change as they're often deeply rooted within you. These beliefs may have been with you since childhood, and they may have been reinforced throughout your life. So, though the circumstances and experiences in your life may cause your self-esteem to fluctuate, you may have a common baseline to which your self-esteem eventually returns, and this baseline is constructed by your solidified beliefs about yourself. For example, your self-esteem may increase for a period after you receive top grades in an exam, but eventually, it may recede to lower levels due to your beliefs about yourself. Maybe you believe that you don't deserve to feel good about your achievements, or maybe you think that you only did well because the test was easy or others didn't try hard. Whatever your negative beliefs about yourself are, if they fuel your low self-esteem, then your self-esteem will invariably return to its low levels no matter the circumstances in your life.

Expanding on your understanding of self-esteem, there are several key elements that make up self-esteem. These elements are, as mentioned, self-acceptance and self-love. Other than those two, there are also self-confidence, feelings of security, a sense of identity, a sense of belonging, and feelings of competence. Self-confidence can help your self-esteem as you will trust in your own abilities more. You will understand your strengths and weaknesses and have realistic and kind expectations toward yourself in terms of performance. Feelings of security can increase your self-esteem as you won't feel too vulnerable all the time. A sense of security can come from a happy and stable family life, financial stability, strong social networks, and so on. These things can comfort and support you in times of need, so you will feel less scared, doubtful, and threatened by whatever life throws at you. Instead, you will feel confident and assured in the face of threats and uncertainty, thus heightening your self-esteem. Having a sense of identity is also good for your self-esteem. If you're unsure of who you are or who you want to be, you may become disconnected, unassertive, indecisive, and lost. But when you have a strong sense of identity, you will know with certainty who you are, who you want to be, what your goals are, and what your strengths and weaknesses are. All this self-knowledge will give you a firm foundation on which to confidently stand, thus increasing your self-esteem. Knowing who you are can also help you like yourself more as you understand yourself deeply and are more able to change the things you don't like about yourself. The next element of self-esteem is a sense of belonging. Humans are social creatures and necessarily place value on social connections. When you feel like you belong in a certain place or group, you will feel connected, safe, and accepted. Finally, feelings of competence can increase your self-esteem as everyone will feel good knowing that they excel or are skilled at something. Knowing your strengths and abilities will improve your self-perception, and you will begin to trust and like yourself more.

Now that you understand what self-esteem is let's discover why it's important. Self-esteem is affected by how you view, value, and like yourself. These simple aspects can impact your decision-making process, emotional health, overall well-being, and relationships. When you have low self-esteem, you will feel more uncertain about your abilities and have more self-doubt. This doubt can color your decision-making process and lead to less-than-ideal outcomes. Your emotional health and overall well-being will decrease with low self-esteem as you will not like or approve of yourself. When you don't like yourself, you will be filled with anger, disgust, sadness, jealousy, and various other emotional poisons that will decrease your happiness. You won't even take the time or energy to take care of yourself, which may harm your overall well-being. These emotions and habits will then harm your relationships. If you can't like yourself, you may not be able to accept that you are liked by others and thus sabotage any healthy and good relationships that you may have. You may even have trouble expressing your needs in a relationship, which can lead to various issues.

Your self-esteem also influences your motivation and assertiveness. When you have healthy self-esteem, you will fully understand your own potential and thus feel inspired to face and overcome new challenges. When you have low self-esteem, you may give up before you've even started due to your negative beliefs about yourself. If you constantly tell yourself that you can't possibly achieve your goals, then you will be much less motivated to try new things or pursue your dreams. On another tangent, if you have healthy self-esteem, then you will be able to assert yourself confidently, stand up for yourself, and ask for the things that you want. This is because you like yourself and view yourself as someone who is worthy and valuable. You will believe that you don't need to put up with bad treatment and that you should chase the things that you want. But if you have low self-esteem, you will have a hard time being assertive and thus often be taken advantage of or lose out on the things that you want. You may believe that you don't deserve to get what you want or that you should accept whatever treatment you're given. Self-esteem is also important as it can help you recognize your strengths and be kind to yourself. When you have healthy self-esteem, you will have realistic and rational views of yourself. This means that you will know your strengths and weaknesses. However, when you have low self-esteem, your self-perception will be skewed and irrational. You may emphasize your weaknesses and reject your strengths. Moreover, when you have healthy self-esteem, you will be kinder to yourself. When you make mistakes, you will learn from them, accept them, and move on. You won't blame yourself unfairly for things out of your control. But with low self-esteem, you will always be unkind to yourself. The second you make a mistake, you may obsess over it, beat yourself up, and blame yourself for everything (whether it was your fault or not).

Moving on, now that you know how important self-esteem is and are hopefully feeling more convinced to improve it, let's see the factors that affect self-esteem. Certain factors that influence your self-esteem are out of your control. For example, age (some people base their self-esteem on their age), genetics (certain genes that you inherit may code for healthier or less healthy levels of self-esteem), disability, and illness. So don't beat yourself up just for having low self-esteem. This is a counterproductive act. Instead, focus on things that are within your control. Life experiences are said to be the most vital factor in self-esteem. For example, you may have developed low self-esteem after being constantly bullied, ridiculed, or critically and negatively assessed by your family and friends. Or you may have developed healthy self-esteem after growing up in an environment that offered you unconditional love and acceptance. No matter your life experiences, they've probably shaped your self-esteem. But now that you're aware of how they're affecting you, you can take control of the narrative, change how you react toward your past, and shape your self-esteem in healthier ways. Other factors that affect your self-esteem are your thoughts and comparisons. If your thoughts are always negative and self-deprecating, then your self-esteem will obviously follow the same pattern. And if you're always comparing yourself negatively to others, your self-perception will plummet, as will your regard and acceptance for yourself. So take control of these elements and try to shape your thoughts and comparisons to improve your self-esteem rather than damage it.

There are endless variables that may affect self-esteem, and these vary from person to person. Something that may severely harm one person's self-esteem may have no effect whatsoever on the next person. So, it's important for you to reflect and discover for yourself what elements in your life are helping or harming your self-esteem. As a general guide, here are the common factors that are widely associated with self-esteem:

- Having a committed partner, a tight-knit family, or a stable workplace may improve your self-esteem.
- Having a healthy and strong relationship with your work (such as gaining identity or meaning from it) may increase your self-esteem.
- Having higher education and a higher income is related to high self-esteem. In the same way, having low socioeconomic status is related to low self-esteem.
- Having a mature and emotionally stable personality is linked to high self-esteem.
- Having social norms about your body and exercise habits imposed on you is linked to low self-esteem.
- Having goals that you choose for yourself and that make you feel fulfilled is linked to high self-esteem.

Other than these factors, social media plays an important role in your self-esteem. Generally, frequent usage of social media is linked to low self-esteem. This is not to say that social media inherently harms your self-esteem. Many people can improve their self-esteem through social media by using it to connect and interact with others in a healthy and happy way. Social media is merely a tool, so the key difference is how you use it—you can use it to build or destroy your happiness. Social media becomes a tool of destruction when you use it to compare yourself with others in terms of work, relationships, or life in general. It's easy to make these comparisons with social media, but you may forget that social media doesn't give you a realistic representation of the lives of others. What you're seeing is a carefully curated and painstakingly constructed version of their lives that is specifically meant to present themselves in the best possible light. You will rarely see the failures, disappointments, or sadness that undoubtedly accompanies every person's life. Instead, you will only see the good news about people's happiness, achievements, and accomplishments. So, it's easy to start to feel bad about yourself when you spend more time on social media. You will start comparing yourself to others which will lead to feelings of inadequacy, jealousy, and resentment. All these emotions are toxic to your self-esteem. So, it's important to remember that every life has its ups and downs. What you see on social media is not the whole picture. And you shouldn't be comparing yourself to others anyways. Everyone has their own unique circumstances, so it's an inherently unfair comparison to make. The only objective and fair comparison you can make is to compare yourself with yourself. This is a much more sustainable way to motivate yourself. But coming back to social media usage, this passage doesn't intend to demonize social media. Moderate social media usage can be good for your self-esteem as long as you remind yourself to use it mindfully and keep a good perspective about it.

Lastly, let's dive deeper into the nuances between healthy, low, and excessive self-esteem. When you have healthy self-esteem, you will be able to avoid dwelling on past negative experiences, believe that you're equal to everyone else (not better or worse than others), express your needs and be assertive, feel confident, say no when you want to, recognize and accept your strengths and weaknesses, and have a positive outlook on life. You will also know that you have healthy self-esteem if you are motivated to reach your goals. This will be because you're able to navigate life knowing what you're capable of. You will believe that you can accomplish your goals, and this will push you to try harder. You will also have healthier relationships as you will be able to assert your wants and needs and set appropriate boundaries with others. This will help you maintain happy and healthy relationships not only with others but with yourself as well.

Meanwhile, low self-esteem may cause you to always believe that others are better than you, be more hesitant about expressing your needs and wants, overemphasize your weaknesses and mistakes, have an intense fear of failure, reject any compliments or positive feedback, have difficulty saying no and setting boundaries, experience fear, self-doubt, and worry constantly, have a negative outlook on life, feel a lack of control often, place others' needs before your own, and have low self-confidence. Having low self-esteem may even lead to several mental health disorders, such as anxiety or depression. You may lack the motivation to pursue your goals, find it hard to maintain healthy relationships, experience a lower quality of life, and be more at risk of suicidal thoughts.

On the other end of the spectrum, excessive self-esteem can be harder to spot as it may often disguise itself as healthy self-esteem. But if you know the traits to look out for, you can easily distinguish between the two. Excessive self-esteem may manifest itself by leading you to be preoccupied with being perfect, always focus on being right, believe that you can never fail, think that you're more skilled or better than others, have grandiose ideas, and severely overestimate your skills and abilities. When you have excessive self-esteem, your relationships may suffer as you must always be in the right, and you may overemphasize their weaknesses to make yourself look better. You will also be unable to accept criticism which will make you more close-minded.

WHAT IS SELF-ACCEPTANCE?

Now let's move on to self-acceptance, an important trait that can help you improve your self-esteem. Self-acceptance is quite self-explanatory—it simply means completely accepting yourself as you are. True self-acceptance is unconditional. If you find yourself thinking, *I'll be able to accept myself more once I achieve this or change this about myself*, then it's not real self-acceptance. Only when you embrace all of who you are, without any qualifications, conditions, or exceptions, can it be termed true self-acceptance. In more specific terms, self-acceptance is your acceptance of all your attributes (including both positive and negative ones). You must accept all facets of yourself, both good and bad. Of course, you may find it easier to accept what you deem good, positive, or valuable about yourself, but this is not enough. You must also embrace the negative, ugly, and less desirable parts of yourself. This will definitely be challenging because those parts are the parts you may desperately want to change about yourself. But rest assured that accepting those parts doesn't mean you now become complacent about them and stop trying to change or improve them. In fact, accepting your negative parts is the only way for you to truly begin the process of meaningful and effective self-improvement. If you're trying to change one part about yourself, but you don't fully accept it as part of your identity, then you're fighting a confusing battle where you're trying to change something that you're telling yourself isn't there. However, once you accept every part of yourself, you will be able to calmly approach the negative parts with love and kindness, and this will make the self-improvement process much less distressing. So you must first acknowledge that you have undesirable traits and habits before you can effectively start on your journey to improvement.

Self-acceptance occurs when you can recognize your weaknesses and flaws, but you still fully accept yourself. Everyone has flaws, so you shouldn't expect yourself to be the perfect exception. Once you accept yourself, including your flaws and past regrets, you will feel more satisfied and at peace with yourself. There are many other benefits to self-acceptance. For example, you will experience an increase in your happiness, positive emotions, sense of freedom, autonomy, self-worth, and self-esteem, and a decrease in your depressive symptoms, desire for external approval, fear of failure, and overly critical inner voice. You can reap all these benefits from self-approval because it is intrinsically linked to your mental well-being. The way you feel about yourself plays a big role in your emotions. When you accept yourself completely, you will feel better about who you are, more comfortable with yourself, more certain of your skills, more motivated to chase your goals, and freer to do as you wish. You will also be more able to control your stress and anxiety, which may prevent you from focusing too much on your weaknesses, mistakes, and regrets. Having higher levels of self-acceptance will even increase your likelihood of conducting acts of self-love, which will then further improve your mental well-being.

To say a bit more about true and unconditional self-acceptance, you must focus on realistically viewing both your strengths and weaknesses. If you overemphasize or underemphasize either of these things, then you will not achieve true self-acceptance. The easier part of this is to realistically accept your strengths. When you win an award, get a good job, or are in a healthy relationship, reflect on your achievements and give yourself the credit you deserve. The harder part comes when you must accept your weaknesses. When you're at your lowest and all your faults and flaws are being pointed out to you, try to view them realistically. No one flaw can decrease your value as a person or completely ruin your future. And no flaw is unalterable or unfixable. Try to keep these things in mind as you come face-to-face with your imperfections. This may make it easier for you to accept them. Other than realistically viewing your strengths and weaknesses, unconditional self-acceptance entails understanding that you're distinct and separate from your actions and qualities. Yes, you have strengths and weaknesses. Yes, you accept them. But no, those strengths and weaknesses don't define you. You have both achievements and failures, skills and flaws, and none of these things alone can define you. This attitude can help you accept that you're fallible and less than perfect. You will be able to accept yourself without judgment when you perform well and when you mess up.

To understand self-acceptance more so that you know what you're striving toward, here are some examples that can show you what self-acceptance looks like. Overall, you can be confident that you've achieved self-acceptance when you can look in the mirror at yourself and accept every little bit of what you see makes you who you are. You will no longer try to ignore, reject, mitigate, or explain away any perceived flaws or faults (be it physical, mental, emotional, and so on). But this can be a bit too abstract for you to catch, and anyway, self-acceptance can look different for each person. So here are some examples of how self-acceptance may express itself within different people:

- Someone going through a divorce may feel like a failure because they couldn't make their marriage work. Self-acceptance for this person may be acknowledging that they made some mistakes and that their marriage failed, but simultaneously recognizing that this one failure doesn't make them a failure, nor does it define them.

- Someone struggling with an eating disorder may be obsessed with their physical figure and hate the way they look. For this person, self-acceptance may look like accepting themselves as a human being with an inherently imperfect body. This person may learn to recognize how they have harmful habits and thoughts and commit to healing themselves.
- Someone who studies hard but doesn't get the grades they desire may feel like they're stupid and worthless. For this person, self-acceptance may be realizing and accepting that taking tests isn't their strong point. They may learn to be okay with this fact about themselves since they have other strengths.
- Someone with low self-esteem may actively ignore and avoid addressing their self-doubt and self-defeating thoughts. For this person, self-acceptance may be confronting all their negative beliefs and cognitive distortions and realizing that their thoughts are harmful and not always true.
- Someone who is a dedicated employee may struggle to meet the demanding goals and deadlines set for them. For this person, self-acceptance may be realizing that they may sometimes fail to deliver but that this failure

doesn't detract from her worth and value as a person and as an employee.

Now that you know what self-acceptance may look like take some time to reflect and discover what self-acceptance may look like for you specifically. Once you do that, you can explore the various ways that you can improve and nurture your self-acceptance. Here, you will learn about several methods to nurture this trait. After you've reflected on how self-acceptance may manifest itself for you, you will be more able to choose which of these methods applies the most to you. Firstly, celebrate your strengths. This is a good way to be realistic about your abilities. Sometimes people may try to downplay their strengths, but this only breeds false humility and an unfair assessment of their competency. Next, understand that you will make mistakes and try to focus on the silver linings in negative situations. Mistakes are unavoidable in this life, so you must learn to make the best of your situation. If you make a mistake, don't beat yourself up. Rather, try to learn from it. Or try to find the silver lining because there will always be one if you care to look for it. Also, develop self-compassion, especially in difficult times. When you're kind and understanding to yourself, you will be more willing to accept yourself. You can even practice staying positive by writing notes of affirmation to yourself or downloading an app for inspirational quotes every day. Staying positive is important for self-acceptance as you will be able to calmly and rationally approach your weaknesses. If you're more inclined toward negativity, then any mistake or flaw you see in yourself may spark more negative feelings, such as anger, sadness, denial, and so on.

Furthermore, don't compare yourself to others, as this is a surefire way to breed self-rejection. When you're constantly thinking that you should be as smart as this person or as athletic as that person, you increase your negative thoughts about yourself, and this will hinder your self-acceptance. To nurture your self-acceptance, try to set an intention of shifting your thoughts from those of blame, shame, and doubt to those of tolerance, trust, allowance, and acceptance. Consciously make an effort to change how you think. Many of your thoughts breed self-rejection, so try to become aware of these and start redirecting your thoughts to those that breed self-acceptance. In addition to putting in the work yourself, you can utilize the people around you by surrounding yourself with people who accept and believe in you. Their acceptance will act as a guide for your own mind, and you will slowly become more accepting of yourself. You can also talk to those around you about how you're feeling. This can help you work through any negative thoughts about yourself and help you see how you can accept yourself more.

When your harsh inner critic is harming your self-acceptance, try to silence that voice with a mantra. For example, *I'm doing the best that I can right now*, or *My flaws and mistakes don't define me*. This can help you feel more at peace with yourself. You can even make a list of all the things you've accomplished and the challenges you've overcome. This can help you feel more capable and worthy whenever you're feeling down. An important method of nurturing self-acceptance is to forgive yourself. Acknowledge the mistakes you've made and hold yourself accountable for them. Reflect on what you learned from those experiences, then let them go. Stop ruminating over the past that you can't change, and simply forgive yourself. Speaking of the past, you can allow yourself to grieve over your regrets and unrealized dreams. But ultimately, you must let go of the past and accept who you are now. Finally, you can try

Positive Emotion Refocusing Technique (PERT) to increase your self-acceptance. To do this exercise, take three long and slow breaths and focus your attention on your stomach. Then bring your attention to your heart while you think of something wonderful that you have in your life. For example, a loved one, a pet, your favorite song, some kindness you gave or received, a place that inspires you, or any other gift in your life. Hold this feeling in your heart and continue to breathe until you feel calmer. Ask this calmer part of yourself if you can better handle whatever situation you're facing. The response you create will invariably be more helpful than the reaction you had when you were upset.

WHAT IS SELF-LOVE?

Finally, let's learn about self-love, another important trait that can help increase your self-esteem. Self-love is simple to understand—it's just the unconditional love you show yourself. Think about the people that you love and how you treat them. Self-love is treating yourself in much the same way, without considering your strengths, weaknesses, traits, or attributes. Your love and care for yourself shouldn't be contingent on your performance or skills. You should love yourself unconditionally. From another perspective, self-love is how you appreciate yourself, and it is a trait that grows from your actions that support your growth (be it physical, mental, or spiritual). Self-love means that you prioritize your own well-being and happiness, so you take care of your own needs and don't sacrifice your well-being to please others. As with self-acceptance, self-love can look different from person to person as everyone has their own ways of taking care of themselves. So here are a few examples of what self-love can look like:

prioritizing yourself, talking to yourself with love, not being overly critical about yourself, giving yourself breaks when you need them, trusting yourself, being true to yourself, setting healthy boundaries, and forgiving yourself. Aside from these, there are many other ways to practice self-love. For example, try to listen to your body so that you're more attuned to what you need in the moment, connect with others, do something creative, eat healthily, and accept yourself.

Other ways to practice self-love are to be more mindful (that is, become aware of what you think, feel, and want) and take action based on your needs. This will help you avoid the automatic and negative behavioral patterns that may harm you, perpetuate your low self-esteem, and lessen your self-love. You may also try to practice better self-care. Show yourself how much you love yourself by taking better care of your daily and basic needs. Try to do things that are good for you, such as getting better sleep, eating healthily, exercising more, and having healthy social interactions. You can even try to recalibrate how you motivate yourself to do things. Most people do things to get them done or because they have to. But now, try to do things because you care about yourself. For example, most people see doing the groceries as a chore, something they need to get done. Try to think about it in new terms. You're doing the groceries because you want to care for your nutrition better. This can foster the thoughts and habits of self-love.

There are many reasons to practice self-love as there are endless benefits to be gained. Self-love can significantly benefit your emotional health. When you exhibit behaviors of self-love, you activate the same areas of your brain's reward system that romantic love activates. This will produce positive feelings within you, such as self-trust, self-confidence, comfort, and peace. As a result, you will tend to experience fewer symptoms of mental health disorders. Having self-love will also result in greater resilience as you know that no matter what, you love yourself and will do your best to take care of yourself. When you have the assurance that you matter and that you're loved, you will be stronger mentally, and you will be more able to pull through whatever life throws at you. When you have self-love, you will feel more secure as you're confident that you've loved and that this love won't go away. This security can increase your self-esteem, self-worth, independence, and autonomy as you won't be shackled by your fears. You will feel safer and more supported when you act on your own and try new things. You will even be more willing to form secure attachments to others. Some people avoid forming attachments for fear that the love they get from that connection will fade or break. But when you have self-love, you will be more open to receiving love from others as you are secure in the knowledge that even if that love goes away, you still have the solid foundation of your own self-love to catch you. Self-love can even affect how you view your mistakes. Instead of beating yourself up over your mistakes, self-love can lead you to acknowledge your mistakes, forgive yourself, and continue loving yourself anyway. This will teach you that your mistakes don't define you and that no one mistake can ever make you unworthy of love. This will then make you more comfortable making your own choices as even if you mess up, you can learn from them and move on without worrying about your worthiness of love. Overall, self-love can motivate you to make healthier choices in life so it can improve your general well-being.

HOW DO THEY ALL RELATE?

In this section, you will receive little reminders of the concepts you've learned so far, and you will gain new insight into how they all relate to each other. Firstly, self-esteem is basically what you think of yourself. Your self-perception affects your self-esteem, and this perception can fluctuate according to your life's ups and downs, but your solidified beliefs about yourself will set the baseline to which your self-esteem will usually return to. Self-acceptance is how much you accept all of yourself, your strengths, and your weaknesses. Instead of comparing yourself to those around you (in positive or negative ways), you instead can appreciate your own unique individuality. Unlike self-esteem which fluctuates, self-acceptance is steady and unconditional. Another distinction between these two concepts is that self-esteem refers to how you feel about yourself (if you assess yourself to be good, valuable, competent, and worthwhile) and self-acceptance is merely the acknowledgment and recognition that you are who you are. Self-esteem often hinges on external factors such as your performance and skills to assess how much you like yourself while self-acceptance is a more global affirmation of self. With self-acceptance, you accept the good and the bad, and you accept that all those parts make up who you are. Self-acceptance can lay the groundwork for healthy self-esteem, but the two are different aspects of how you think and feel about yourself. Self-love comes from the dedication, practice, and effort that you put into loving yourself unconditionally. These three concepts differ from each other in that self-esteem is an evaluation of yourself, self-acceptance is an attitude you adopt toward yourself, and self-love combines both actions and feelings where you feel affection for yourself and put that affection into action by caring for yourself.

However, you need all of these concepts (the evaluation, attitude, actions, and feelings) to really improve your self-esteem. If you have good self-esteem but no self-love, it is contradictory. You may like yourself and evaluate yourself positively, but you won't love yourself so you won't take good care of yourself. This lack of self-love will eventually poison your self-esteem. In the same way, if you have good self-esteem but no self-acceptance, your self-esteem will gradually decrease. You may evaluate yourself positively, but you won't be able to accept your flaws or strengths. This will continue to skew your self-perception until eventually your self-esteem is lowered. So as you're working on your self-esteem, remember to concurrently focus on your self-acceptance and self-love. In the next chapter, you will learn more about self-doubt, which is a trait that can harm your self-esteem.

Chapter Two

THE ROOTS OF SELF-DOUBT

Now that you understand the concepts of self-esteem, self-acceptance, and self-love, let's explore a common reason why you may find yourself lacking these traits: self-doubt. This is a negative trait that can diminish your confidence, kindness, trust, and perception of yourself. When you have high levels of self-doubt, you will have trouble trusting yourself. You will constantly question whether you deserve good things, whether your achievements are true reflections of your skills, whether others like you, and whether you're a person of value. Specifically for self-esteem, self-doubt can be like a parasite that robs you of a healthy self-perception. There are many factors that may contribute to your self-doubt and harm your self-esteem. This chapter will give you detailed explanations of common issues that make it harder for you to believe in yourself. Understanding what may be raising your self-doubt (and thus lowering your self-esteem) may provide you with more perspective as you study and use this workbook.

One prevalent root of self-doubt is past shame.

Everyone undoubtedly has some embarrassing memories from their past or things they've done that they now regret. Such memories can elicit feelings of shame. So, let's try to understand shame more. This feeling can make you feel like there's something wrong with you. This is different from feeling like you've done something wrong (that feeling is guilt). Rather, shame comes from the underlying belief that you're not good enough. For example, you may constantly recall a past event where you didn't perform as well as you wish you had. This may cause you shame because you feel like that performance says something negative about your worth as a person. Or you may have been bullied, ridiculed, ostracized, or told that you're weird and this made you feel shame. This emotion can be connected to any past experiences you've had where you felt embarrassed, insecure, or inadequate, or where you were self-doubting and self-critical. The feeling of shame evolves throughout your life. Through your own thoughts, emotions, and behaviors—and the negative reinforcement, words, and actions of others—shame may have become part of your identity. You may constantly recall past experiences that you deem negative in order to label, stereotype, criticize, stigmatize, and judge yourself as not good enough. When you dwell on your past shame, they become more than just past events, they transform into the lens through which you interpret yourself and the world around you.

This is how low self-esteem may be sustained by shame. If you're consistently dwelling on your past humiliations, you are feeding and reinforcing that small voice in your mind that tells you lies, such as that you're unworthy of love, not skinny enough, not smart enough, not rich enough, not skilled enough, and overall, simply not good enough. And if you keep telling yourself these self-deprecating lies, your self-perception will plummet, your self-esteem will be damaged, and you will lose all motivation to try to be more than you think you are. The effects of shame are the exact opposite effects of self-worth, self-love, and self-esteem. While the latter traits can help you feel worthy, valuable, and loved, shame only makes you feel worthless and unlovable. You will believe that you are inherently bad or without value, thus crushing your self-esteem. So it's important to learn how to let go of your past. Holding onto them will only harm your self-esteem and happiness. Instead, learn what you can from those experiences and once they don't help you anymore, let them go.

There are a few factors affecting how shame may affect you. The first is the timeline of your shameful event. Often, people may hold onto shameful events from their early life or key life moments. If you were shamed as a child, you might have built your belief systems and values around that event. For example, if you were shamed for being too loud when you were first learning about curiosity and play, this shame may affect you even now as you forgo that curiosity and prefer to be submissive and silent. Or, if you were shamed by your friends for not having the latest toys and gadgets, you may now be more sensitive toward shame around poverty and wealth. Another factor that changes how shame may act upon you is gender. The typical gender roles and attributes may cause you to feel shame if you don't conform to the norms. Men are usually attacked for being vulnerable, as this is wrongly perceived as a weakness. This shame around vulnerability may prevent men from seeking mental health care. In a nuanced way, women are also shamed for being too emotional and hormonal. This may cause women to try to suppress their true emotions for fear of being labeled crazy or irrational. There are countless ways in which society can shame you, and every story of shame and stigmatization affects your self-worth and self-esteem. Currently, you may try to cope with your shame by numbing yourself (through food, addiction, social media, and so on), conforming excessively to social norms and expectations (such as fixing anything and everything that you may be shamed for and trying to meet all the ideals enforced on you), or putting on a show for others to see (such as buying things you can't afford or feigning confidence on social media). But these are all unhealthy and temporary solutions to the wider problem of shame. These methods only keep your low self-esteem at bay and play at imitating high self-esteem. But true self-worth and self-esteem will never be accomplished as long as you keep buying into the narrative that you and society keep enforcing to yourself: that you're not good enough or worthy if you're not a certain way. This belief hinges your value and self-perception on unstable and mutable things, which is not a healthy foundation for your self-esteem. So, in order to address your past shame effectively and build up healthy self-esteem, you must work through all the distortions that your shame is telling you about yourself. Separate the identity that your shame has built for you and the identity you really have. This can help you embrace your self-worth and increase your self-esteem. As you address your past, you will slowly come to realize that you are enough.

Other than past shame, your family of origin is another common root of self-doubt. Your family of origin is simply the family you grew up in (as compared to the people that you currently live with who may not be the same). Your family of origin plays a pivotal role in your development as this is where you learn how to communicate, process your emotions, and get your needs met. Many of your values and beliefs will have been instilled in you by your family, and you will have developed your sense of self in the context of your family of origin. Your self-esteem relies heavily on what type of family of origin you had. Supportive families create an environment that nurtures your self-esteem. Everyone supports one another, encourages each other's strengths and talents, and keeps one another grounded and well-adjusted. Unsupportive families damage your self-esteem by frequently criticizing each other, pointing out each other's flaws, and manipulating each other. In these kinds of families, children may have difficulty cultivating independence and autonomy, thus making it hard for them to develop their self-esteem.

On another tangent, your sense of self (which is vital for your self-esteem) is also greatly influenced by your family of origin. Children who are shown love, kept safe, and offered stability typically develop stronger senses of self—compared to those who don't. Children whose needs for love, safety, and stability are often unmet may develop senses of self that are weak or damaged, resulting in low self-esteem. There are endless ways in which your family of origin may have impacted you. All families have negative and positive parts as well, and any and all of these aspects may have an effect on your current life. If you grew up with a family of origin that was dysfunctional (witnessing and experiencing issues such as abuse, alcoholism, poverty, and poor health) and didn't provide you with real-world skills, you may experience hardships in these areas as you grow up. Therefore, you may sincerely doubt your ability to live as a high-functioning individual, decreasing your self-esteem. And if your family of origin didn't show you how to properly express love, you may have dysfunctional relationships in adulthood, further decreasing your self-esteem as you can't figure out why your relationships have all suffered. But it's not all negative. Sometimes, you may develop good coping strategies or relevant strengths in the face of a dysfunctional childhood. However, without awareness of how your family of origin may affect you, you will probably repeat the negative patterns you observed growing up. So, to overcome the possible negative effects that your family of origin may have on you, you must reflect on all the ways it may be harming your self-esteem, find a way to accept your childhood, and focus instead on your present moment. The key here is not to place the blame on anyone but to simply accept that your childhood happened in the way that it did and that it's now time for you to release the hold it has on you.

On a related note, childhood trauma can cause you to have extremely high levels of self-doubt well into your adult life. As a child, you learn to value yourself from the actions, words, and reactions of others, especially those closest to you such as your parents and friends. These people give shape to the way you perceive yourself as a child and can later influence your self-esteem and self-confidence as an adult. Childhood trauma can break the trust you have in your parents and caregivers (who in your mind were the ones supposed to protect you) and thus give you no foundation on which to build your self-esteem. Instead, this trauma can make you feel worthless, despondent, scared, and unstable. All this will damage your sense of self which in turn will lower your self-esteem. Childhood trauma can be understood as any situation, event, or series of events that occurred during childhood that overwhelmed you and made you feel like you couldn't cope. These events may be physical or emotional and real or perceived, as long as they triggered your fight or flight response which may have affected how you viewed and experienced life from then on. For example, if you grew up surrounded by violence, addiction, or abuse, you will have learned from an early age that you cannot trust people (and this effect is heightened when you're witnessing violence, addiction, or abuse with your parents who are the ones meant to protect you and give you a sense of stability and security) and that the world is a dangerous place. This lack of trust and fear of the world may increase your self-doubt and lower your self-esteem. Childhood trauma also increases your feelings of powerlessness as you can't do anything to change those circumstances. This may then lead to feelings of shame, guilt, low self-worth, high self-hate, and low self-confidence. You may even develop avoidant coping mechanisms (such as withdrawal, isolation, and self-criticism) to deal with all these emotions, which will only further exacerbate your self-doubt and low self-esteem.

Moving onto factors occurring in the present, your negative thoughts may play a role in your self-doubt. These negative messages about yourself may have been learned when you were young, but they're being actively reinforced and sustained in your present. Previously, you may have learned these negative thoughts from others, such as your teachers, family members, or the media. Maybe your teachers told you that you were stupid and hopeless. Maybe your parents told you that you were fat. Whatever the negative message, you may have repeated that message to yourself over and over, especially whenever you weren't feeling well or were going through a hard time. Over the years, as you constantly repeated these messages to yourself, you may have come to believe in them, thus damaging your self-perception. You may have even gotten into the habit of saying negative things to yourself and added some negative messages or thoughts of your own.

This will worsen the problem, making you feel even worse about yourself and lowering your self-esteem. The dangerous part of having negative thoughts about yourself is that no matter how untrue, unsupported, or unrealistic they are, you may tend to believe in the truth of those messages. The second you mess up or are having a bad day, your mind may become flooded with thoughts that you're stupid, unworthy, unlovable, and so on. Your negative thoughts often assume the worst of yourself, and you may believe those thoughts since you've grown so accustomed to them. You may not even be aware of them anymore, and thus, these negative thoughts can be hard to unlearn. This is doubly dangerous as a lack of awareness of your negative thoughts will allow them free reign to strengthen and multiply. This will only increase your self-doubt, lower your self-perception, and decrease your self-esteem. So pay attention to your thoughts and guide them to more positive, realistic interpretations. Jot down your negative thoughts whenever you notice them and then take a closer look at them. This may help you realize that your negative thoughts aren't as accurate as you automatically assume. When you're in a good head space, look back on the negative thoughts you've written down and ask yourself if the message is really true, if a person would or should say this to another person (and if not, why are you saying it to yourself), and what you get from thinking this thought. This can help you gain new perspectives on your negative thoughts.

Another common root of self-doubt is perfectionism. This is where you strive to make everything perfect, whether that's yourself, others, or life in general. You have unrealistic expectations about how things should be, and you have a hard time letting go of those ideals and accepting how things really are. There are several drawbacks to perfectionism that contribute to low self-esteem and high self-doubt. Firstly, you tend to ignore your own accomplishments. Perfectionism values end results over everything, including the amount of effort you put in. With this mindset, you may ignore a lot of your own accomplishments. You may have put in an enormous amount of effort but if things don't go exactly your way you may still feel like a failure. This will lower the trust you have in yourself and blatantly ignore all your hard work. Next, perfectionism can hurt your relationships. One type of perfectionism is socially-prescribed perfectionism where you believe that others have very high expectations of you so you may constantly be afraid that others won't think that you're good enough. This can harm your relationships as you may always feel like a disappointment to others and always clamor for their validation and approval. Other than that, perfectionism can cause you to forget what defines you. No one can ever be defined by a single thing. Humans are complex, nuanced, unique creatures that often defy definition. But when your mind is trapped in perfectionism, you may place too much emphasis on your job, your relationships, your wealth, your body, and so on. You may become hyper-focused on one specific area, or even one specific instance, and decide that it's life or death —you must be perfect or everything will fall apart and you will be worthless. In reality, whatever your perfectionism is focusing on right now is just one part of your life. It's not the entire picture, and it most certainly can't define you. You may also develop a bad habit of quitting before you get started. You may think that if you can't be the best or if you can't do something perfectly, then it's better that you don't try it at all. This can limit you and prevent you from trying a variety of new things. More importantly, this can prevent you from getting that self-esteem boost when you complete a task, achieve a goal, or try something new. This will keep your self-esteem at its low levels.

Perfectionists also have a hard time accepting compliments and this will keep their self-esteem levels low. No matter how hard you work or how well you perform, you will tend to focus on the small details that weren't perfect. This prevents you from recognizing your accomplishments and allowing the praise of others to boost your self-esteem. Your unrealistically high standards stop you from seeing yourself in a positive light. Another effect of perfectionism that damages your self-esteem is that you compare yourself to others. Comparing yourself to others is inherently an unjust comparison to draw as everyone has different circumstances, strengths, weaknesses, and skills. Perfectionists take this one step further and make even more unbalanced comparisons. For example, if they're a beginner at something, they may compare themselves to experts who have years of experience with them. This will serve to emphasize to them how they're lacking in perfection. However, it's an unfair comparison to make if you're comparing your first attempt to someone else's hundredth attempt. Perfectionists often make such comparisons to criticize themselves or motivate themselves to try harder. But such comparisons are unnecessary and ineffective. All that is needed is more time and practice.

Moreover, abandonment issues are a prevalent cause for self-doubt and consequently low self-esteem. Parents are meant to be positive role models for their children. For example, a son needs his father to show him how to relate to the opposite sex and how to relate to others as a man. Without a father figure, boys may grow up and experience difficulties forming close relationships with people, especially romantic relationships. Anyone who has been abandoned may develop a very negative mentality about themselves, believing that they are to blame for being abandoned, that they somehow deserved to be abandoned, and that they were abandoned because they are worthless. It's easy to see how such beliefs can lead to high self-doubt and low self-esteem. After being abandoned, you may feel like others didn't value you and this can increase your distrust of others and yourself (you may start to doubt yourself, your skills, and your worth). This would then decrease your self-esteem.

The final possible root of self-doubt is a desperate desire to please others. This often comes from having a low opinion of yourself (that is, low self-esteem) and the behavior it invites often emphasizes, reinforces, and sustains that low opinion of yourself. If you're a people pleaser, you may already have low self-esteem and thus draw your self-worth from the approval and validation of others. You may think that others will only like and care about you if you're useful, so you may bend yourself backward trying to get their praise and appreciation so that you can feel good about yourself. Another trait of being a people pleaser is that you often spend time worrying about being rejected. This fuels your need to please others. If they're never displeased with you, then they'll never reject you. So, you start to do anything in order to keep those around you happy. You may even experience strong desires to feel needed as you believe that others will like you better if you're useful to them. If others need you, they may be nicer to you and offer you more affection. This may make it hard for you to say no as you worry that doing this will make you lose their favor or make them believe that you don't care about them. So, you simply agree with whatever others ask you to do, even if you don't have the time, energy, or desire to help. As a people pleaser, you're always placing the needs of others before yours, and this may make you vulnerable to being exploited. Others may ignore your boundaries because they know you'll cave into their requests anyway.

Those are the typical traits of a people pleaser. Now let's discuss how those traits affect you. It's good to take into account what others want, need, and feel. These traits usually come from a place of affection and concern. But you must be careful to take into account your own needs and feelings. Often, people pleasers leave out this part and only consider the feelings and desires of others. This makes them easy to manipulate and abuse as they're always putting others ahead of themselves. This can be tiring for them as they're always going out of their way to help others. And, in a way, they're putting on an act in order to gain approval and validation. They're not being true to themselves and how they feel, choosing instead to do whatever will make others happy. This isn't exactly honest and will eventually harm your relationships with those who sincerely wish the best for you. Your relationships with others will definitely suffer if you're a people pleaser. You may feel frustrated, tired, and resentful to others if they don't recognize and appreciate your sacrifices. This may lead you to display passive-aggressive behavior, which may confuse or upset others, especially those who aren't intentionally taking advantage of you. These are the common roots of self-doubt, which is a trait that can easily harm your self-esteem. In the next chapter, you will learn how to deal with your self-doubt using cognitive behavioral therapy (CBT).

Chapter Three

A COGNITIVE BEHAVIORAL THERAPY APPROACH TO SELF-DOUBT

The key takeaway in this chapter is that self-doubt can be combated using the principles of cognitive behavioral therapy (CBT). In order to equip you to achieve this, you will learn in simple language the principles that back up CBT, how they can be applied in overcoming low self-esteem, and finally the various steps of practically using CBT to improve both your cognition and behavior to improve your self-esteem.

UNDERSTANDING COGNITIVE BEHAVIORAL THERAPY

CBT is a type of psychological treatment that explores how your thoughts, emotions, and behaviors interlink. It's commonly held that a distressing trigger or situation can cause you to have negative thoughts, which can lead to negative emotions and physical distress, which can then cause you to exhibit negative behaviors. So, the main focus of CBT is to teach you how to alter your thoughts (your cognition) and your actions (your behaviors). There are three posited levels of cognitions that are addressed through CBT: core beliefs, dysfunctional assumptions, and automatic negative thoughts. Your core beliefs are learned and influenced by your experiences in early childhood. Being formed in your childhood means that these beliefs are deeply rooted in your belief system and significantly influence and define the negative views you have about yourself (for example, thinking that you're worthless and that you hate yourself), the world around you (for example, thinking that others don't like you or that no one cares about you), and the future (for example, thinking that things will never get better or that you're going to be a failure). Dysfunctional assumptions are cognitive distortions that occur when you overly focus on the negatives. This biased perception can distort how you view reality and lead to badly misinterpreted information. Dysfunctional assumptions are irrational thought patterns that are exacerbated by your negative thoughts and emotions. Finally, your automatic negative thoughts are the involuntary negative perceptions of your situations that occur out of habit. You may have formed these habits growing up, and now you no longer notice when they occur. However, these fleeting and automatic negative thoughts can cause negative emotions to occur. The way to overcome these thoughts is to alter and reframe them more rationally and positively.

Before you learn the exercises and skills of CBT that you can use to address your self-doubt, you must familiarize yourself with the principles of CBT so that you know how to effectively administer this treatment on yourself. There are eight main principles that underlie CBT:

- CBT is based on an ever-changing and ever-evolving formulation of the patient's problems and an individual conceptualization of each patient in cognitive terms. This is why CBT is best done with a therapist. A mental health professional would be able to effectively identify your current thinking patterns and problematic behaviors, making sure to consider your past experiences and childhood. They would then be able to form a conceptualization of the patient based on the information provided to create an accurate picture of the patient's situation. This is helpful for the treatment process as a mental health professional would be able to give valuable insight and perspective. However, CBT can still be conducted on your own. Just make sure to self-reflect often to form your own conceptualization of your entire situation. And try to be as objective as possible.
- CBT is goal-oriented and problem-focused. You must set specific goals for yourself so that you can evaluate and respond to the thoughts you have that interfere with and hinder those goals.
- CBT initially focuses on the present. Treatment should initially focus yourself, on your current problems that are causing you emotional or physical distress. CBT only delves into the past once you've gotten stuck in a negative pattern or dysfunctional thinking that may stem from your past. Trying to understand your past can help you understand and modify your current core beliefs.
- CBT is educative and emphasizes relapse prevention. By teaching you the skills and

knowledge you'll need to be your own therapist, CBT endorses long-term healing as you will be able to sustain your progress and improvement on your own. CBT will teach you how to understand your inner processes, how your thoughts impact your feelings and actions, how to identify and evaluate your thoughts and beliefs, and how to plan for behavioral changes.
- CBT strives to have a time limit. The goal is to eventually get to a point where you don't need constant therapy anymore. Though you will always make use of the skills and knowledge you've gained, CBT ultimately aims to make you self-sufficient and independent.
- CBT is structured to maximize efficiency and effectiveness. The typical structure that you can follow as you conduct CBT on yourself is to follow the introduction–middle–final model. For the introduction, do a mood check, briefly review how your week was and set an agenda for the session. For the middle, review last week's homework, discuss the problems on the agenda, set new homework, and summarize. For the final part, give yourself feedback on how you think this CBT is working for you.
- CBT teaches you how to identify, evaluate, and respond to your unhealthy, maladaptive, and dysfunctional thoughts and beliefs. Once you identify these things, you will be more capable of questioning them, analyzing them, and replacing them with more realistic and rational perspectives. You may even create behavioral experiments to directly test the validity of your thoughts.

- CBT teaches you many problem-solving techniques that can change your thoughts, moods, and behaviors. The types of techniques that are most effective for you will vary based on your personality, objectives, and situation, so be patient as you try to find the right CBT techniques to help yourself.

Overall, all these principles are aimed at helping you alter your negative thoughts and actions to be more realistic and rational. You will learn how to identify your problems, build awareness of your negative thoughts and actions, recognize that your thoughts are just opinions and not the truth, distinguish between facts and thoughts, consciously challenge and reframe your dysfunctional assumptions, set achievable goals, be more present, be kinder to yourself, develop a more positive outlook on life, be more resilient, be more in control of yourself, be your own therapist, and prevent any relapses. These are all the things you can expect to learn as you embark on CBT. Aside from these beneficial skills, there are many other positive aspects of CBT. Namely, CBT can be completed in a relatively short period of time, can help treat symptoms of mental illnesses without relying on medication, can alter your thoughts and behaviors to enact real changes in how you feel, can teach you practical strategies that can be applied in your daily life, and can help you be more proactive in your own life. However, there are also a few disadvantages to CBT. These are that CBT requires you to play an active and committed role which can demand a lot of your time and energy. CBT also involves confronting your anxiety and uncomfortable emotions, which may make you more hesitant to embark on this journey. But all that can be said for this is that any therapy is bound to be uncomfortable, but it is necessary and worthwhile in order to lead you to greater happiness and mental health. So, now that you're well versed in what to expect of CBT let's start learning some exercises.

COGNITIVE BEHAVIORAL THERAPY EXERCISES

The first CBT exercise is called 7 Steps, and it aims to challenge thoughts that support low self-esteem. This is a fairly simple exercise and, as the name suggests, it only takes seven steps:

- Identify a common negative message that you repeat to yourself. For example, you may tell yourself that you're a failure, that you're unworthy of love, that others don't like you, and so on. Write this particular thought down onto a sheet of paper and try to notice if this thought is triggered by a specific problem, situation, or stressor. For example, you may often feel like a failure during exam season, or you may often feel like others don't like you during social gatherings.
- Ask yourself if there's an aim or goal for this thought. Is this thought trying to help you or protect you in any way? How is this thought helping or protecting you? Maybe this thought helped you in the past by preventing you from being vulnerable or from taking an unwarranted risk. However, this doesn't mean that this thought is still helping you in the same way now. Honor the fact that this thought has

helped you in the past but remain objective about whether or not it's still helping you now.
- Look for evidence against your negative thoughts. If your negative thought tells you that you're a failure, look at all the things you've accomplished or the things that you're good at. If your negative thought tells you that you're unlovable, look at all the people who do love you. Aside from looking for evidence against your negative thoughts, try to find (tangible and objective) evidence for your thought. If you can't find any, then you can safely assume that the thought isn't supported. If you can find some, try to question them. Is this the whole story? Are you being fair and objective?
- Ask yourself what a wise and fair version of yourself would say about this. For example, your wise self may say that it's not fair to say that you're a general failure or that you fail all the time since there are a lot of examples of you doing well and excelling at things.
- Find a new role for your inner critic. Your inner critic is the source of your negative thoughts, but it's not inherently harmful. In fact, criticism is meant to protect you and help you grow. But often, your inner critic may get out of control and not perform this role well anymore. So, redirect your inner critic and help it help you. Tell your inner critic that it can protect you and motivate you to do better, but that negative thoughts aren't the effective way to do that. Instead, teach your inner critic to notice the things you're doing well and to use a kind and

compassionate tone when noting the things you can improve on.
- Try to come up with a more helpful thought that you can believe right now. For example, once you've disproved the negative thought that tells you, you're a failure, try to replace it with something more positive. Thinking that you're a success or excelling may be a bit hard for you to believe at the moment so try to find a positive message about yourself that you can believe, such as that you may fail sometimes, but you're trying your best, and sometimes you succeed.
- Remind yourself of this new thought and reinforce it until you can easily believe it. To help you with this step, you can write it down as a reminder to yourself on your phone or leave little notes to yourself around your room. Reiterate this message to yourself often, and soon enough, it will become a habit. You will slowly get better at believing this new thought, and eventually, it will replace your old negative thought.

The second CBT exercise you will learn is a gratitude journal. This can help relieve your self-doubt by making you more aware of all the things you have to be grateful for in your life. When you're more cognizant of the good things in your life, you will become more confident and more willing to view yourself positively, thus increasing your self-esteem. You can write in your gratitude journal in the morning to reflect on the previous day or at night to reflect on the same day. Try to be consistent with your schedule so that it becomes a habit. The first version of a gratitude journal is to simply write down the highlight of your day. Common highlights are having dinner with friends or loved ones, talking to a friend, going to the gym, eating a good meal, or watching your favorite movie. Another version of a gratitude journal is to write down three positive aspects of your day. To help you think of three positive aspects, you can try to fill in these sentences:

- One good thing that happened to me today is …
- Today I saw someone do something good when …
- Today I saw something good happen to someone when …
- Today I had fun when …
- I smiled today when …
- Something that I will always want to remember about today is …
- Someone that I was thankful for today was …
- Something interesting that happened today was …
- Today I achieved …
- Something funny that happened today was …
- Today was special because …
- Today I'm proud of myself because …
- My favorite part of today was …

The next CBT exercise to address your self-doubt and self-esteem is called Strengths Exploration. If you know your strengths and are able to acknowledge and recognize them, then you will have more success in several areas, and this will in turn lower your self-doubt and improve your self-perception. You will be happier and more likely to accomplish your goals. Below is a list of common strengths. Read through this list and circle the ones you think apply to you. Feel free to add more strengths to this list as this is not an exhaustive list.

- Flexible thinking: you can see that your thoughts are not always truths and you can unhook from your thoughts when they're unhelpful.
- Respect: you can look up to others who have knowledge, wisdom, or advice.
- Teamwork: you're good at working with others.
- Problem-solving: you can see the problems you have as challenges instead of threats, and you can put in the effort to solve your problems.
- Appreciating beauty: you can appreciate art, music, dance, theater, paintings, and other expressions of beauty.
- Grateful: you can recognize the good things in your life and feel thankful for them.
- Love: you can express and receive love.
- Growth: you emphasize change and improvement.
- Kindness: you can forgive others and yourself and treat others well.
- Enthusiasm: you love what you do and have a passion for things.
- Friendship: you are a good friend to others.
- Honesty: you don't lie, keep your promises, and can tell people openly about the things you care about.
- Curiosity: you find the world very interesting and like to experience new things.
- Focus: you can pay attention and concentrate when you want to. You can react mindfully

when something excites you or raises strong emotions or urges.
- Leadership: you can take charge and help a group work well together.
- Humor: you can make others laugh and brighten their day.
- Social intelligence: you can fit into various situations and can empathetically sense how others are feeling.
- Love of learning: you love to learn new things and grow.
- Humility: you can accept when you're wrong and when you're not the best at something.
- Persistence: you can keep trying at something even when it seems difficult.
- Self-control: you're highly disciplined and can stick to your goals despite temptations.
- Courage: you can overcome fear, uncertainty, or intimidation when you think that a goal is worthy.

Once you go through this list and add any relevant strengths you think you have, explore how you can use these strengths more in your daily life and how you can utilize your strengths to solve your problems and overcome obstacles in your life.

Following this, the next CBT exercise aims to reward yourself with positive self-talk. It's important to mind how you talk to yourself. Previously, you learned how to challenge your negative thoughts. Now, you will learn how to flip the script and talk positively to yourself. Change your negative thoughts into positive ideas. Determine the root cause of your negative thoughts and come up with a positive solution or message to tell yourself about it. For example, if you think that you're too stupid to do well on a test, you may discover that the root cause of that thought is your doubt about your ability to retain what you study. The positive message you can create from this is, *I can take this step by step, learning the material slowly and steadily to improve my chances of success.* If your negative thought is that nobody likes you, you may find that your underlying worry is your doubt that you're a likable person. The positive message you can get from this is, *My close friends all think that I'm a likable person as they enjoy spending time with me.* Or your worry might be specific to a single person not liking you. For this, you can tell yourself, *This person may not like me but it's just one person. This doesn't mean that I'm not likable in general.*

The final CBT exercise helps you set healthy boundaries. Personal boundaries are the rules and limits you set for yourself within relationships. Healthy boundaries help you take care of yourself and avoid uncomfortable situations. For this exercise, remind yourself that you have basic rights. These basic rights that apply to everyone are:

- The right to say no without feeling guilty or having to deal with others getting angry.
- The right to be treated with respect.
- The right to have your needs be just as important as the needs of others.
- The right to make mistakes.
- The right to not meet the unreasonable expectations of others.

If you have weak boundaries, you may sacrifice your personal goals, values, and plans to please others or allow others to define who you are and make your decisions for you. Whereas if you have rigid boundaries, you may find it hard to open up to others and relate to them. So as you try to figure out what your boundaries are, make sure you stay away from weak or rigid boundaries. Healthy boundaries will vary depending on the type of relationship (work, friends, family, romantic partners, and so on) but generally, they will allow you to feel safe, respected, and balanced. These are all the CBT exercises that can help you address your self-doubt and increase your self-esteem. In the next chapter, you will move on to learning about positive psychology and how it can help you.

Chapter Four

THE POWER OF POSITIVE PSYCHOLOGY

This chapter will focus on how you can engage with positive psychology to upgrade your sense of self-worth. In order to do this, you must first understand both of these concepts. Positive psychology has been described in various ways with countless words, but the general definition of this field of psychology is that it is the scientific study of what makes life most worth living. This brief explanation can be elaborated on if you see positive psychology as a scientific method of studying human emotions, behavior, and thoughts. This method of study focuses on human strengths rather than human weaknesses, on building up the good in life rather than repairing the bad, and on upgrading an average life into a great life rather than only focusing on improving a bad life into normal, average life. These aims of positive psychology mean that this field highlights the positive influences and occurrences in life, such as positive experiences (joy, happiness, love, inspiration, and motivation), positive states and traits (resilience, compassion, empathy, and gratitude), and positive institutions (that support you and apply positive principles within them). Within this field, you will spend much of your time considering topics such as your character strengths, life satisfaction, optimism, joy, gratitude, compassion, self-compassion, well-being, self-esteem, self-confidence, hope, and self-improvement. By focusing on these topics, positive psychology believes that you can learn how to better flourish and live your best life.

UNDERSTANDING SELF-WORTH

Obviously, positive psychology can benefit you in many ways. However, as previously stated, this chapter will mainly focus on one way in which positive psychology can benefit you. That is its effect on your self-worth. Now, you've already studied the concepts of self-esteem, self-acceptance, self-love, and self-doubt. These are all useful concepts to understand as you try to navigate your way toward higher self-esteem. Self-worth is another important concept for you to grasp as it can supplement your self-esteem. Self-worth refers to how much you value yourself and believe that you are worthy. Self-worth is essentially the feeling you have that you are a good person who deserves to be treated with dignity and respect. This presence or absence of this feeling can affect how you act toward yourself and how you feel about yourself in comparison to others. This is a vital trait to have as it ensures that you treat yourself well and with respect. Like many of the other concepts you've learned, self-worth may seem similar or even indistinguishable from self-esteem. But they are two totally different concepts. They may interlink and act on one another, but they are two fundamentally separate traits. There are nuances between the two concepts that set them apart from one another.

Self-esteem is what you think, feel, and believe about yourself. It's your self-perception based on your core beliefs and certain life experiences. Meanwhile, self-worth is the recognition that you are greater than the sum of all those things. Despite what you think or feel about yourself and any negative experiences you may face, self-worth will provide you with the wisdom to acknowledge that you're not defined by any of those things. You will have a deep knowledge that you are a person of value, deserve love, are necessary for this life, and have inherent, incomprehensible worth.

Since this chapter aims to enhance your self-worth, let's study this concept a little deeper so that you know what you're striving toward and how to best approach it. Self-worth exists at the very core of your sense of self. Your thoughts, emotions, and actions are all intimately tied to how you view your worth and value as a person. This is why, according to the self-worth theory, an individual's main goal in life is to achieve self-acceptance. This self-acceptance is often found through achievement which in turn is often found through competing and comparing yourself with others. According to this theory, competing with others can make you feel like you have impressive accomplishments to add to your name. This can help you feel more confident and prouder of yourself, which will enhance your acceptance of yourself and your estimation of your own value. Expanding on this theory, it is held that there are four main elements to the self-worth model. These elements are ability, effort, performance, and self-worth. The first three elements interact with each other to determine the last element (self-worth). Your ability and effort usually have a big impact on your performance, and even when the outcome isn't as desired as you want it to be, you may be able to acknowledge how hard you worked and how that effort has improved your ability. In this way, all three elements contribute to your feelings of worth and value. This theory represents a realistic understanding of self-worth as the majority of people tend to approach it. People tend to see their self-worth as tied to their accomplishments, achievements, and performance. This isn't necessarily unhealthy or ineffective as long as you keep in mind that your performance and achievements are only supporting factors to your self-worth. You should never tie your self-worth to things that are so subjective and fluctuating. Your self-worth is a constant, steady, stable, and innate thing. So, it does become unhealthy and ineffective when you see your self-worth as inextricably linked to your achievements and accomplishments. This type of mindset places too much emphasis on your performance and can lead you to several maladaptive habits and beliefs, ultimately resulting in low self-worth.

Other than basing your self-worth on your accomplishments or on competing and beating others, there are various other factors that you can use to contribute to your sense of self-worth. However, as with the previous factor of accomplishments, you must be wary and always remember that these factors should only contribute to your self-worth—they must never define or control it. When you base your whole self-worth on something external, then your sense of self-worth becomes very vulnerable and mutable. So remember that all these factors can help your self-worth, though they should never be able to significantly damage it. That being said, these are the common factors that people use to enhance their self-worth. The first is your appearance. This can be measured by your weight, clothing size, and the kind of attention that you receive from others. It's easy to allow this factor to become toxic so remember to approach your appearance in a realistic, kind, healthy, and balanced way. The second factor is net worth, such as your income, financial assets, or material possessions. Being able to provide for yourself and your loved ones is a positive attribute, so many people use their net worth to boost their self-worth. However, be careful that this doesn't spill over into greed, jealousy, coveting, or pride. Try to remain grounded and humble even as you recognize your financial accomplishments. The third factor is your social circle. Your friends and the people you surround yourself with can make you feel valuable or worthless. So be mindful of whom you choose to spend your time with. The fourth factor is your career. If you're in a career with good prospects and good pay, and if you're passionate about the work that you do, your self-worth will improve. You will feel like you're living a good life.

To clarify, your job is not your career, and your career is not your job. A job is a short-term position with short-term goals such as earning money. A career centers around your long-term goals; is the sum of all your possible jobs in a given field and can help you build a satisfying and fulfilling life. This distinction is necessary so that you don't fall into a common misconception about self-worth. Many people believe that their job plays a role in their self-worth and thus feel compelled to stick it out and stay at a particular job that they're not enjoying and that doesn't fulfill them. This misconception can cause you a lot of grief, unnecessary pain, and wasted time. No one job can or should impact your self-worth. A job is just a job. There will always be the next one and the next one. Rather than focusing on sticking it out with this one job, you should instead be focusing on shaping and pursuing your career. By doing this, you can control the direction of your life and shape it to be more fulfilling.

While on this subject, let's dispose of other common misconceptions about self-worth. There are many things that shouldn't determine your self-worth. Firstly, your to-do list. Many people like to feel productive. Of course, being productive is a positive trait, and it always feels good to achieve your goals and cross things off a list. However, your to-do list and daily levels of productivity don't have a direct relationship with your worth as a human. You can be very productive today and less productive tomorrow, and your value as a person will have stayed the same. A prevalent misconception about self-worth, especially in this day and age, is that it can be tied to your social media following. While it's nice to know how many people think that you're worth following or like what you have to say, being followed, liked, retweeted, or reposted online doesn't impact your worth as a human being. It's good to be open to the considered, honest and informed opinions of others, but at the end of the day, the opinions of others should have no impact on your own personal, innate sense of self-worth. Another unhealthy measure of self-worth that people use (especially as they get older) is age. You may feel like you're too young or too old for certain things, but you must remember that your age is simply a number. It's something completely out of your control, and it's a natural part of being alive. So, why should it affect your value as a person?

As there are several ways for you to erroneously approach self-worth, let's dispose of a few more misconceptions before moving on. You may be using other people as a measure of your self-worth but, as mentioned above, the opinions of others shouldn't affect your self-worth. Rather than focusing too much on what others are thinking, saying, doing, or achieving, you should focus on your own personal fulfillment, satisfaction, and goals.

Moreover, you may be measuring your self-worth by your physical abilities. While it's good to be in shape and perform well at physical activities, you should approach these things with joy and the aim of improvement rather than the aim of determining your self-worth. If you place so much pressure on your physical performance, you may overstress yourself and compromise your performance. So instead, aim to keep improving and allow yourself to feel joy and fulfillment. This will increase your general well-being and happiness. The same goes for your intellectual performance. Some people hinge their self-worth on their grades, but the reality is that everyone has strengths and weaknesses. Just because your strength or weakness happens to be test-taking or memorization doesn't make you any more or less valuable than the next person. An honor student has the same amount of value as a high school dropout. This is because everyone's worth is innate and inherent; it can't or shouldn't be affected by anything external.

Previously, you read that your social circle can factor into your self-worth. This only means that the people you hang out with can make you feel better or worse about yourself, so you should be mindful of who you choose to be in your social circle. It has been said that the opinions of others shouldn't affect your self-worth, but realistically they will have an influence, no matter how small. So, to avoid unnecessary damage to your self-worth, you should be careful about who you listen to and who you spend your time with. A misconception that can come from this is that you may start to define your self-worth by how many friends you have. But your value as a person has absolutely nothing to do with your connections or number of friends. For friendships, try to remember quality over quantity. If you have two friends that make you feel good about yourself and that support each other, that's a great deal better than having 20 friends that make you feel bad about yourself. In the same vein, your relationship status isn't a positive or negative comment on your value. Whether you're single, married, or dating (casually or committed), your value is the exact same. Another misconception that may arise is that your money can determine your self-worth. Previously, it was said that your net worth could contribute to your sense of self-worth. Many people may take this to mean that the more money they have, the more value they have. This is completely missing the point. Using your net worth to contribute to your self-worth only entails recognizing, appreciating, and giving yourself due credit for being able to provide for and possibly treat yourself and your loved ones. This is a loving, responsible, and fulfilling thing to do. But if you think that having more money gives you more value, then you will never be satisfied no matter how much money you have. Finally, your hobbies and likes don't affect your self-worth. Some people are shy about their interests as they worry about having good taste and sophistication. But these things don't affect your self-worth so just be open about what you like. You may find others who share your interests. The main thing to remember as you're trying to increase your self-worth through positive psychology is this: no one, not others and not even yourself, can detract from your worth. Your worth is inherent and innate, it isn't affected by anything external; it is simply something that you have deep within you. If you believe that you're valuable and worthy, then you are valuable and worthy. If you don't believe that you're valuable and worthy, you're still valuable and worthy! Your worth exists undeniably and immutably within you—you just have to find and accept it.

POSITIVE PSYCHOLOGY EXERCISES

The first positive psychology exercise to help you develop your self-worth aims to increase your self-understanding. The more you know who you are, the more willing you may become to accept your inherent worth as a person. You must learn who you are and what you want in order to be more open to deciding that you're a worthy human being. To do this exercise, simply conduct this thought experiment on yourself: imagine that everything you have is suddenly gone or stripped away from you. All your possessions, relationships, friendships, career, jobs, status, money, accomplishments, trophies, certificates, and so on are now gone. Give yourself some time to really imagine what this would look like and feel like. Then, ask yourself these questions:

- What if everything I have is suddenly stripped away from me?
- What is all I have left is just myself?
- How does this make me feel?
- What do I really have left that is of value?

Write down your answers and take some time to think about them. Try to see if you can reach this conclusion: no matter what happens to me externally and no matter what is taken away from me, I'm not internally affected. Return to your thought experiment and test out this conclusion. No matter what external things get taken from you, your internal being is not affected. Once you can conclude this, try to ask yourself these next, deeper level of questions:

- Who am I? Who am I not?
- How am I?

- How am I in the world?
- How do others see me?
- How do others speak about me?
- What important life moments define or affect who I am today?
- What makes me feel the most passionate, fulfilled, and happy?

These questions can help you explore and discover who you are and what parts of your life bring you satisfaction and joy. Try to focus on these answers more and find ways to enhance those areas that are bringing you positivity and light. Then, to round off your self-understanding, you must ask yourself questions to find the more negative parts of your life:

- Where do I struggle the most?
- Which areas can I improve?
- What fears do I have that often hold me back?
- What emotions often hurt me?
- What mistakes do I tend to repeat?
- Where do I constantly feel disappointed or let myself down?

These questions are necessary for you to have a balanced, realistic view of yourself and your life. You must be aware of the things in your life that can potentially obstruct your positivity and happiness. Next, in the spirit of positive psychology, you will return to looking at the positives in your life. Ask yourself:

- What skills and abilities do I have?
- What do I excel at?
- What are my positive attributes and strengths?

Give yourself enough time to reflect and consider every question, especially the questions that remind you of your worth and value as a person.

The second positive psychology exercise aims to boost your self-acceptance. Once you accept all of who you are as a person, you will be more able to accept that you have inherent worth. It's best to do this exercise after the previous one. It's easier to accept yourself once you have a better grasp of who you are. For this exercise, think about the mistakes you tend to make and repeat. Then try to forgive yourself for those errors. Think also of any struggles, room for improvement, lapses in judgments, and bad habits you have. Spend some time committing to forgiving yourself for all those things. Accept yourself without making excuses for yourself or judging yourself. Remember that everyone has flaws and imperfections and that your weaknesses are just a part of who you are. If you're struggling to forgive yourself and accept your flaws, try to repeat the following statements to yourself:

- I accept everything about myself—the good, the bad, and the ugly.
- I fully accept every part of myself, even including my fears, flaws, habits, and qualities that I'm not too proud of.
- This is how I am, and I am at peace with that.

The third positive psychology exercise aims to enhance your self-love. Having more self-love will make it a lot easier for you to accept that you have innate and inherent worth. Following the two exercises that have increased your self-understanding and self-acceptance, this exercise helps you build love and care for yourself (all of yourself, including the parts of yourself that you don't like so much).

This exercise aims to heighten your kindness, generosity, compassion, and tolerance of yourself. To do this, you simply need to pay attention to the tone you use when talking to yourself. Many people aren't aware of their tone, and thus they cultivate hostile, critical, and negative head spaces for themselves. This environment isn't conducive to self-love. So, try to commit to being more positive and uplifting when you talk to yourself. Once you change your tone, your mind may become a more positive, friendly, loving, and caring space. This will facilitate your self-love which in turn will increase your self-worth. If you're not sure how to use a loving tone with yourself, try to repeat these loving affirmations to yourself: *I am valued; I am unique; I love myself with all my heart; I am a worthy and capable person.*

The fourth positive psychology exercise asks you to recognize your own self-worth. Once you understand, accept, and love yourself, you will be more aware and willing to accept that your self-worth doesn't and shouldn't depend on others, your performance, or any other external factors. At this point, you're in the best position to recognize that your worth is innate and to appreciate yourself for all the work you've put in to get to this point. You will also be able to continue maintaining your self-understanding, self-acceptance, self-love, and self-worth. To do this exercise, simply set aside some time every day to reflect on your self-worth and to repeat some affirmations to yourself. Remind yourself that you no longer need to please other people, that you alone can control how you feel about yourself (regardless of what other people do or say and regardless of anything external that happens to you), that you have the power to respond to situations and circumstances (due to your internal skills, sources, resources, strengths, and resourcefulness), and that your value comes from inside and it can never be diminished.

These affirmations and reminders should help you recognize and accept your own worth.

The fifth positive psychology exercise focuses on self-worth again to help you solidly bring about a steady sense of your own worth. This is a sentence completion exercise that only takes a few minutes to complete. It gives you a chance to write about yourself and reflect on the positive parts of your life. To do this exercise, simply fill in the following sentences:

- I was really happy when …
- Something that my family and friends like about me is …
- I'm proud of …
- My family was happy when I …
- In school, I'm good at …
- Something that makes me unique is …
- I feel excited and passionate when …

These prompts will encourage you to think about the things that make you who you are. You will be led to reflect on what you like, what you're good at, and what makes you happy. Focusing on these positive aspects of your life utilizes positive psychology to help you build a happier life.

The sixth positive psychology exercise is simply to take responsibility for yourself. While it's great to have self-love, self-worth, self-understanding, and self-acceptance, it's equally important to remember that, even as you achieve inner peace and happiness, you must still practice responsibility, accountability, and integrity for yourself, your issues, and your situations. To do this exercise, try to apply the following guidelines in your life:

- Take full responsibility for whatever is happening to you so that you don't give your personal power, agency, and autonomy away.
- Acknowledge that you have the personal power and will to change and affect the situations and events happening in your life.
- Remind yourself of the self-love, self-worth, self-understanding, and self-acceptance that you have worked so hard to attain. This can help you remember that you hold the power in your own life.
- Enjoy and appreciate your well-deserved sense of self-worth and remember to maintain it as you go about your daily life.

The last section of this chapter will simply equip you with positive quotes to help you live into the theory of positive psychology more fully in your life. These quotes can give you an idea of the mindsets you should be striving toward, or they can serve as positive affirmations that you can repeat to yourself on a daily basis to remind yourself to be positive and to accept your own worth. The following positive quotes are taken from various people and have been compiled by Peter Economy (2018):

- You yourself, as much as anybody in the entire universe, deserve your love and affection.
  —Buddha
- Self-care is never a selfish act—it is simply good stewardship of the only gift I have, the gift I was put on earth to offer to others. —Parker Palmer
- Why should we worry about what others think of us, do we have more confidence in their

opinions than we do our own? —Brigham Young
- Love yourself first and everything else falls into line. You really have to love yourself to get anything done in this world. —Lucille Ball
- Remember always that you not only have the right to be an individual, you have an obligation to be one. —Eleanor Roosevelt
- If you could only sense how important you are to the lives of those you meet; how important you can be to people you may never even dream of. There is something of yourself that you leave at every meeting with another person. —Fred Rogers (Mr. Rogers)
- What lies behind us and what lies before us are tiny matters compared to what lies within us. —Ralph Waldo Emerson
- A healthy self-love means we have no compulsion to justify to ourselves or others why we take vacations, why we sleep late, why we buy new shoes, why we spoil ourselves from time to time. We feel comfortable doing things which add quality and beauty to life. —Andrew Matthews
- People may flatter themselves just as much by thinking that their faults are always present to other people's minds, as if they believe that the world is always contemplating their individual charms and virtues. —Elizabeth Gaskell
- Until you value yourself, you won't value your time. Until you value your time, you will not do anything with it. —M. Scott Peck
- Never be bullied into silence. Never allow yourself to be made a victim. Accept no one's

definition of your life; define yourself. — Harvey Fierstein
- Too many people overvalue what they are not and undervalue what they are. —Malcolm S. Forbes
- Remember, you have been criticizing yourself for years, and it hasn't worked. Try approving of yourself and see what happens. —Louise L. Hay
- Act as if what you do makes a difference. It does. —William James
- You're always with yourself, so you might as well enjoy the company. —Diane Von Furstenberg
- The better you feel about yourself, the less you feel the need to show off. —Robert Hand
- One's dignity may be assaulted, vandalized and cruelly mocked, but it can never be taken away unless it is surrendered. —Michael J. Fox

Choose a few of these quotes that apply the most to you and write them down as reminders to yourself. This can help keep you on the right path to higher self-worth and self-esteem. In the next chapter, you will learn more about perfectionism, which is a common thief of self-esteem.

Chapter Five
PERFECTIONISM NO MORE

UNDERSTANDING PERFECTIONISM

Perfectionists find it very hard to appreciate their own efforts or those of others and may find themselves battling low self-esteem due to not meeting up with their unrealistic, rigid standards and expectations. This chapter explains how you can escape from perfectionism. To help you determine if you are indeed a perfectionist, there are 12 common signs of perfectionism.

- You allow no room for mistakes. When you see an error (no matter how small), you immediately want to jump on it and correct it.
- You have a very specific way in which you want things to be done.
- As long as something is out of place or doesn't conform to your standards, approach, or expectations, you can't accept it. This can make it hard for you to work with others.

- You have an all-or-nothing approach where you either do something perfectly or not at all.
- You're overly focused on the end result. Anything that happens in between (such as the effort you put in) is irrelevant to you. All that matters is achieving the goal.
- You feel annoyed, devastated, or distressed when you can't achieve your goal or perform perfectly.
- You're extremely hard and unforgiving to yourself. It doesn't matter if it's your fault or not; you will automatically beat yourself up when things go wrong. Or you may feel extremely bad about a mistake you made for a long time.
- You have extremely high, often unrealistic standards. These standards may cause you undue stress and anxiety.
- You may be held back by your impossible standards as you procrastinate and avoid working on your goals because you fear you can't meet your own standards.
- You feel that success is not enough. Whatever you achieve, you usually won't give yourself enough credit and start to aim for something even higher.
- You constantly spot mistakes when others don't. This can mean that you're very observant and detail-oriented or it can simply mean that nothing is ever good enough for your perfect standards. Sometimes the mistakes you see are real while other times they're self-imagined.
- You often sacrifice too much time, energy, and your own well-being to perfect something.

If these signs are applicable to you, then you may be a perfectionist. Though just using the term perfectionist may seem reductive. To expand a bit more, there are three different types of perfectionists: the self-oriented perfectionist, the other-oriented perfectionist, and the socially prescribed perfectionist. The self-oriented perfectionist is typically very conscientious and detail-oriented. They want to get every detail right because they value attention to detail. This can become obsessive and cause undue amounts of anxiety. Other than that, self-oriented perfectionists place high standards on themselves and will be very critical of themselves in many areas of life. Their perfectionist standards are imposed inwardly on themselves. The other-oriented perfectionist is the opposite of the self-oriented perfectionist as their perfectionist standards are imposed outwardly on others. Like self-oriented perfectionists, other-oriented perfectionists have impossibly high and often unrealistic standards, and they are extremely critical. The big difference is that all of this is directed toward others. They are harshly critical when other people fail to meet their standards. This can cause several problems in their relationships and at work. Other-oriented perfectionists usually won't delegate work and will try to do everything themselves because they believe that others just can't get things right. Finally, the socially prescribed perfectionism imposes standards on themselves according to what they believe society expects from them. In order to be seen in a certain way by society, the socially prescribed perfectionist imposes certain standards on themselves. They may be trying to be perfect for their family, friends, or boss, or they may be trying to meet a social standard. This person's self-esteem is linked to how they are viewed by the world.

Speaking of self-esteem, perfectionism has a terrible

effect on how you view yourself. Perfectionism can be channeled in a healthy way to be beneficial for yourself. You can use it to push yourself, motivate yourself, and keep yourself focused. But often, perfectionism is taken to its extreme where it becomes wildly unhealthy. Here are the ways that perfectionism can ruin your self-esteem. Firstly, as a perfectionist, your mind will become wired to constantly see the negative in the positive. Whenever you achieve something or receive praise, you will automatically notice or create a negative aspect to criticize yourself over. This turns something that should be a source of positivity and gratitude into something negative and self-deprecating. As long as something isn't perfect, no matter what you achieve and no matter how much others praise you, all you will see is the one flaw. You will criticize and evaluate yourself negatively, thus struggling to like and accept yourself. Another way perfectionism can harm your self-esteem is by creating a mindset where you have to be the best all the time. People tend to compare themselves with others. It's a hard thing to control. But perfectionists take this to the extreme. When they're sure that they're the smartest, funniest, fastest, wisest, nicest, or most interesting person in a certain group, they can feel assured and confident in themselves. But when you're always trying to be the best, you will inevitably be confronted with the reality that you're not the best at something. And this is when a perfectionist's self-esteem will suffer. Perfectionism may lead you to believe that as long as you're not the best, you're never good enough. Finally, perfectionism can harm your self-esteem as you will tend to take things personally. When you're a perfectionist, any criticism or opinions of others may cause you to become defensive or despondent. You may distort what others comment about you and transform constructive criticism into exaggerated condemnations. This is understandable since perfectionism causes you to be overly self-critical, so it only follows that you will interpret others' comments as critical as well. And when you're always assuming that others think the worst of you, you will begin to think the worst of yourself as well, thus harming your self-esteem.

EXERCISES TO REDUCE YOUR PERFECTIONISM

Now that you understand how dangerous perfectionism is, especially to your self-esteem, let's start learning the exercises you can use to address this trait. The first exercise is a flexibility self-assessment. It's important for you to know how flexible you are in your perfectionist thinking. The less rigid and more flexible you are with your thought patterns, the easier it will be to change and correct your unwanted beliefs. The more rigid and less flexible you are, the harder this will be, so you must become aware of this now and put in more effort to become more mentally flexible. This exercise can help you explore where your thinking is more rigid and where you may want to focus more attention as you strive to escape your perfectionist tendencies. To do this exercise, simply ask yourself these questions:

- Do you find it hard to identify when you're being a perfectionist? Give some examples.
- Do you find it hard to relax your high standards? Give some examples.
- Are you usually unwilling to listen to or consider someone's suggestion that you're being a perfectionist? Give some examples.

- Do you get defensive or typically disagree when someone tells you that your standards are too high? Give some examples.
- Do you get upset or distressed when you can't meet your own standards? Do you get upset when others can't meet your standards? Do you get upset when you feel you didn't meet a certain social standard? Give some examples.

If you find that you're more inflexible with your perfectionist thinking, you must make extra effort to monitor and change your ways of thinking. Over time, you can learn to improve your mindsets.

Another exercise is to identify your perfectionist triggers. There are usually recurring triggers or themes that cause your perfectionist tendencies, thoughts, and habits to emerge. Try to reflect on all the times that your perfectionist tendencies have shown up. Write down all the instances you can think of, then try to find some common themes that link them. This will help you build a better picture of your perfectionism and help you reflect on the activities or situations that may trigger your perfectionism. Come back to this exercise regularly to continue reflecting, adding, or deleting things from your list. As you're doing this, try to identify the areas of your perfectionism where you can cut yourself some slack and the areas of your perfectionism that can really harm your life.

The next exercise is goal setting. The problem with perfectionism is that your goals will always be unrealistic or impossible. Learning how to set goals in a healthy way can help you define the problem you want to overcome and what you need to do in order to overcome it. To do this, you must identify the problems you want to address and list their priority levels. Focus on the higher priority goals first.

Remember to re-write this list regularly to revise the priority levels of some goals and to add or remove goals. Also, remember to set SMART goals. This stands for:

- Specific: Rather than stating a general, vague goal (such as, "I want to get into shape,") state a specific, action-based goal (such as, "I want to go to the gym three times a week.")
- Measurable: Your goals must be trackable so that you can measure your progress at set intervals. This way, you'll be able to observe and appreciate your tangible progress. For example, don't say, "I want to be more active." Say, "I want to run for half an hour, three times a week, for three months."
- Attainable: This is pivotal to your success. You must set goals that are challenging but feasible. Goals that aren't challenging won't motivate you, while goals that are impossible will leave you discouraged and more likely to give up. So, reflect on your abilities and set goals that are high but within reach.
- Relevant: Ask yourself why you're chasing this particular goal and why you want to achieve it. If you can't answer these questions, then perhaps you're chasing the goals of someone else. Your goals need to be relevant and important to yourself in order for you to be motivated, focused, and determined to achieve them.
- Time-bound: You must set a balanced deadline for yourself. If the deadline is too generous, you may become lax and unmotivated to put in the work. If the deadline is too unrealistic and

unforgiving, you may become overstressed and self-sabotage. So, set a realistic deadline that will help you stay focused. Also, be willing to alter your deadlines if unexpected situations occur.

Other than setting SMART goals, there are other tips on setting yourself up for success. Break your goals into smaller steps so that they seem more manageable. This can even create milestones for yourself and achieving these smaller goals will encourage you to keep working hard. Furthermore, celebrate all your achievements. Give yourself small rewards for achieving small goals and plan major rewards for when you achieve your main goal. You will also be more successful if you ask for help from others to hold you accountable for your goals. Your friends and family can offer you emotional support, advice, or a stern hand when you need it. On this tangent, remember to accept compliments. Don't keep looking for the negatives in everything. When someone compliments you, simply thank them and leave it at that.

To end this chapter, let's read through some quotes on perfectionism. These quotes can be used as positive affirmations or convictions against perfectionism. Or they can just frame perfectionism in a new light for you. Use these quotes in whatever way is beneficial for you, but do spend some time considering each quote to gain as much as you can from each one. These quotes are taken from various people and have been compiled by Cristina Morero (2021):

- Perfectionism is the voice of the oppressor, the enemy of the people. It will keep you insane your whole life. —Anne Lamott

- Perfectionism is self-abuse of the highest order. —Anne Wilson Schaef
- Perfectionism is a delusion that can rob one of a very successful, enriching life if not careful. —April Bryan
- Perfectionism is the art of never being satisfied. —Unknown
- Perfectionism means that you try not to leave so much mess to clean up. But clutter and mess show us that life is being lived. —Anne Lamott
- Perfection is a roadblock to progress. —Unknown
- Perfect is the enemy of good. —Voltaire
- People call me a perfectionist, but I'm not. I'm a rightist. I do something until it's right, and then I move on to the next thing. —James Cameron
- I will be patient with myself as I develop into the person I am meant to be. Being perfect is not the goal. Continuing to grow in a positive direction is the goal. —Unknown
- When things are perfect, that's when you need to worry most. —Drew Barrymore

As you use these exercises and quotes to address your perfectionism, try to incorporate the exercises and knowledge you've learned so far about self-worth, self-acceptance, self-esteem, and so on. All these things can help you develop a healthier mindset as you combat your perfectionism. In the next chapter, you will learn about how you can confront your past to increase your self-esteem.

Chapter Six

VENTURING INTO THE PAST FOR BIG REWARDS

This chapter addresses your past experiences and guides you on how you can begin to rewrite your narratives, avoid self-esteem issues due to past negative experiences, and move forward with hope for your future. A common emotion you may come up against as you're venturing back into your past is shame. This sense of shame can come from any number of sources. Maybe you experienced physical, emotional, mental, or sexual abuse, or maybe you encountered certain traumas that instilled a sense of shame within you. Or maybe you blame yourself for something that went wrong in your past. Or you may constantly remember decisions and actions you made that you now regret. You may have acted impulsively and recklessly, bringing harm to those around you. Or you may have been stigmatized growing up for your race, appearance, family, and so on. Whatever the source, shame is a normal and common emotion to face when thinking about your past. It is also one of the most destructive and corrosive emotions. This is because you tend to hide your shame and not share it with others. And like any wound that is kept hidden and not addressed, it only gets worse over time. So before you learn how to address your past, you must first equip yourself with the knowledge of how to cope and heal from shame. This knowledge will allow you to more effectively explore your past and loosen the hold your past has on you. Once you eliminate your sense of shame, you will be able to see things more clearly and objectively.

UNDERSTANDING SHAME

The first step in overcoming your shame is to acknowledge what you're feeling. Sometimes shame can occur in subtle, nuanced ways, so it's not always obvious that you're feeling ashamed. Sometimes this may express itself in the form of anger, irritability, and defensiveness while other times it may manifest itself as depression or procrastination. You must take some time to reflect on yourself and your emotions to identify when shame is driving certain emotions. To do this, simply ask yourself why you're feeling this way. Why do you get defensive when certain topics come up? Why do you get angry when a loved one suggests that you're being a perfectionist? Why do you get depressed when you receive constructive criticism? You may find that you're using these emotions (anger, sadness, defensiveness) to hide your shame. These topics or actions make you feel ashamed so to escape from that shame, you overreact with other emotions. You want to protect yourself from shame or being shamed. But this doesn't solve the source of your shame and only causes more problems in your relationships. So next time, ask yourself if you're acting this way because of your shame. This can help you understand your actions and emotions more and thus allow you to control your reactions better.

Once you're more able to identify when shame is acting upon you, the next step to overcome this shame is to observe it without judgment. This is an extremely hard step because you probably don't enjoy the feeling of shame, so you immediately judge it as dangerous, undesirable, uncomfortable, and so on. You naturally want to push it away, ignore it, reject it, or distract yourself. But the more you try not to think about it, the more you fear it, and the more you refuse to address it, the stronger it will become. Your emotions demand to be felt and if you intentionally ignore them, they will manifest themselves even stronger and in various ways. So rather than judging your shame and consequently avoiding it, allow yourself to feel it. Don't shy away from this emotion; just let yourself experience it and observe it. Where do you feel it in your body? What does it feel like (such as fear or disgust)? What thoughts does it bring about? Be curious about your emotions. The better you understand it, the more control you will have over it and the less scary it will seem to you. One important thing to clarify here is that while you're not judging or avoiding your shame, you're also not feeding it. Sometimes people may feed their shame through harsh self-criticism. This will exacerbate your shame and cause you unnecessary distress. So don't feed your shame. Just experience it as it is.

As you're observing your shame, try to make this important distinction: Are you feeling shame or guilt? These two emotions are very different. Guilt is a useful emotion where your conscience is telling you that you've let yourself down in some way. Guilt can lead you to notice your mistakes, fix them, improve your behavior, and reflect on how you want to be. Guilt is almost always directed toward your actions. This makes it a more productive emotion as you're actively reflecting on how to improve and how to avoid similar mistakes in the future. Meanwhile, shame is usually a comment on your inherent value and thus has a deleterious effect on your self-esteem. Guilt and shame can be applied to the same situation, but the things they tell you are vastly different. For example, if you upset your friend by accidentally saying something hurtful and insensitive to them, your guilt will tell you that you messed up, that you should apologize, and that you should be more careful in the future. Your shame will tell you that you're a horrible, nasty person who doesn't care about others and who always hurts others. Guilt encourages you to improve your behaviors, but shame makes you less able to do so since it suggests to you that you're inherently, irrevocably, and permanently bad. Guilt allows room for growth while shame denies it. So it's important to distinguish between guilt and shame. If you're feeling guilt, be proactive about it and figure out how you can improve yourself. If you're feeling shame, try to switch your thoughts more to the guilt category so that you can approach the past situation more effectively. Switching your emotions and thoughts from shame to guilt can help you actually enact positive change in your habits rather than simply damaging your self-esteem.

It's a lot easier said than done, switching from shame to guilt. To do so, and to move past shame in general, you must develop some compassion for yourself. If you struggle with self-esteem, you're probably often too hard on yourself. You may be able to be compassionate toward others, but you never extend the same compassion to yourself. If you're not sure if this applies to you, do this little thought experiment. Imagine that you treated others the way you treat yourself. You speak to them as you speak to yourself and you criticize them as you do yourself. How would others respond to this? Would you be well-liked?

Would others want to spend more time with you? Would you be ostracized and cut out of friend groups? If the conclusion of this thought experiment is a negative response from others, then you probably could stand to show more compassion to yourself. So rather than treating others like you treat yourself, try to treat yourself the way you treat others. Whenever you identify a source of shame, try to take a step back and stop any automatic thoughts or actions you may be tempted to indulge in. Instead, try to regard and treat yourself the same way you would a friend. Imagine your friend is confiding in you about how they're ashamed for the exact same reason you're currently feeling ashamed. How would you react to them? What would you say to them? Would you comfort or condemn them? How would you try to help them? You would probably treat them with compassion and tell them that they deserve to be happy no matter what flaws they have or mistakes they've made. So try extending this same compassion to yourself. Just as your friend's shame may be decreased through the care and compassion you show them, your own shame can be reduced if you show yourself understanding and compassion.

Another way to overcome shame is to open up about it. As noted previously, shame likes to hide behind other emotions, but this only heightens it. Try talking about your shame to people you trust and love. Sometimes, just saying something out loud can help you heal. Having someone listen to you without judgment can also increase your own self-acceptance and self-love. Having someone respond to you and help you work through your emotions can increase your self-understanding and self-esteem. Once you open up about your shame, you will no longer feel the need to hide it, and this can help you deal with it more directly. You will no longer feel alone, and you will start to feel supported and loved. If you're not ready to open up about your shame yet, that's fine too. You can try writing about it. This simple act can help you acknowledge your shame and explore it in more detail. Shame is a destructive emotion that can harm your self-esteem. It can convince you that you're bad, weak, unlovable, and undeserving. But once you bring shame into the light, you will be more able to acknowledge it and work through it, lessening its control in your life.

HOW TO EXPLORE YOUR PAST

Now that you understand how to deal with shame, a common roadblock as people explore their past, let's discover how to treat your past experiences in a fair and healthy manner. The first skill to acquire is adopting a third person view. Usually, when you recall a memory, you see it from your own perspective, from a first-person view. This may make you overly involved in the memory and emotionally biased. Compared to when you recall things from a first person view, your brain activates different parts once you adopt a third-person, observer viewpoint. This is because you're engaging in a different perspective as you approach your memories, hence different parts of your brain are activated. Memory recall is an active process where you're susceptible to biases and distortions. However, when you adopt a third person view, you guide yourself to view your past in a new way. This requires greater interaction among the brain regions that are involved in your ability to recall the specific details of a memory and to recreate those mental images in your mind. So by training yourself to use a third person perspective, you rewire how your brain interacts to recreate those memories, reducing your vulnerability to biases and distortions. There is even a therapeutic purpose to adopting this perspective. By viewing your past experiences from an observer's standpoint, you can remove yourself and thus reduce the intensity of your emotions associated with that memory. This can make it easier for you to revisit troubling or traumatic memories.

The next skill you need to address your past is self-awareness. Being self-aware can help you discern what you feel toward a certain memory, help you accept that emotion, and ultimately help you move on and live in the present. To be more self-aware, one thing you can do is examine your reactions. As you're remembering your past, try to be aware of your physical and emotional self. See how they respond to certain parts of your memory. This can offer you invaluable information about your inner life. Pay special attention to your body as often your body can give you insights into your mind without your cognitive awareness. Notice if your toes curl, if your brow creases, if your hands clench, if you hold your breath, if you flinch, if you cringe, and so on. Once you notice your reactions, you can ask yourself questions to explore why you're reacting like this. Another way to be self-aware is to keep a dream journal. Your past memories, especially those that you hold onto and that are significantly affecting you even now, may find expression in your dreams. This may not always be obvious; dreams are often strange and inexplicable. That makes it all the more important for you to consciously allow yourself the space and time to go through your dreams which you may not fully understand. Examining and noticing details in your dreams can help you gain a deeper knowledge of yourself. As you sleep, your mind may go through significant past events that you may not even realize are still affecting you. If you see any semblances in your dreams, then try to follow those paths and see where they take you. Your emotions and thoughts about past events may reveal themselves in the safety of your dreams. So keep a notebook and a pen by your bed and write down any dreams you remember as soon as you wake up. The things to note are what happened, how you felt, what you thought, and as many specific details as you can manage (no matter how small or insignificant they seem). Then, reflect on how your dreams may connect to your current or past situations. See if any patterns or themes emerge in your dreams over time.

Keeping a regular journal is important for self-awareness too. Journaling can help you sift through the many thoughts and emotions that you have, bringing to light certain things that are lurking beneath the surface. Writing things down also helps you understand the narratives that you tell yourself, allowing you to safely express and process your own thoughts, emotions, and feelings without any judgment. You can journal after a session of reflecting on your past so that you can sort through all the emotions and thoughts that were brought up. Or you can simply journal every day to take stock of how you are. Or you can use specific prompts to help you reflect on certain topics (such as specific past experiences). Another popular technique for increasing self-awareness is meditation. This exercise asks you to be still and to simply sit with yourself. This can help you encounter the truth of your experiences and help you be more present in the moment. You will be able to notice who, where, and how you are currently and accept all of that without judgment. This is a useful exercise to use when you want to bring yourself back into the present after an intense session of exploring your past. However, it takes a lot of practice to get good at meditation so you should try to meditate regularly. Meditation apps are available to you, and they're very helpful in guiding beginners through the steps and mindsets of meditation. These apps can even help you make meditation a habit. Other than these apps, self-compassion guided meditations are another alternative for you to try. These guided meditations incorporate affirming prompts to lead and focus your meditation practice. Using this guided meditation can help you increase not only your self-awareness but also your self-love.

Another self-awareness practice is to draw out the scenario in your head. As you're recalling a memory, try to put it onto paper. This way, you can consciously construct the memory and see which parts of it are clear and important to you. Having a visual representation of how you view this past event will also help you understand yourself more and your thoughts and emotions toward this past event. Once you've drawn it out, take some time to look at it and scan your body for any physical or emotional reactions. The final self-awareness practice is to focus on your frustrations. When you're exploring your past, it's normal to encounter negative emotions. Not only shame but anger, regret, disappointment, and so on. It's not easy to explore these emotions but doing so can offer you a wealth of insight into yourself. As you're exploring your past and you encounter uncomfortable or distressing emotions, try to write down what thoughts and emotions you're experiencing and what event sparked them. Ask yourself what this event or moment is trying to teach you, why you may have reacted with those thoughts and emotions, what negative habits are being provoked, and how you want to act if this event happens again. After doing this, try to end this period of self-reflection by stating one thing you're grateful for in that situation.

Moving on from self-awareness, another skill you need as you explore your past is the ability to rewrite your narrative. Sometimes, you may become trapped in the same old story that you tell yourself. You may have revisited a particular memory so many times and experienced it in the same way over and over that you've become stuck in your own way of seeing it. Now, it's your job to reshape this narrative that you tell yourself. This is accomplished in five steps:

- Think about three to five important, key experiences that you think have negatively affected your life.
- Consider and write down all the benefits, opportunities, or lessons that have come from those experiences.
- Ask yourself what you currently see as being the cause of those negative experiences. Then, reconsider your answers. Could it be that there are some factors that you don't know? Is there more to what happened than you think? What would it mean if something else had caused this event?
- Consider how these experiences have shaped your outlook on life and the world. Then, reconsider your outlook. If you viewed your past experiences differently, how would this change your outlook on life and the world? How would this change how you feel toward other people?
- Think about how these three to five experiences have shaped your identity and your self-perception. Then, reconsider your identity. Focus on the positives rather than the negatives. How have you grown due to these experiences? What strengths or chances have been made

available to you because you went through those events? How is your future going to be different because you've experienced these things? How have these past events influenced what you're committed to doing and being? How can you use these events to help other people? Given that you've gone through such negative experiences and made it out, what does this say about you as a person? What does this say about your potential and abilities?

If you consider these questions, you will be able to change the narrative with which you frame your past experiences. This can help you change past negative experiences into positive growth opportunities in the present. In the next chapter, you will learn about how to use radical compassion to deal with your harsh inner critic.

Chapter Seven

USING RADICAL COMPASSION TO
SILENCE YOUR INNER CRITIC

This chapter will help you groom your inner voice, which may currently be judgmental, overly critical, and mean, to be more compassionate, understanding, and kind. To do this, you will learn about radical compassion. Compassion by itself can be understood as empathy directed toward the distress of others. Radical compassion is a specific type of compassion that includes an inner imperative to alleviate the pain of others. Alternatively, you can understand this term as total compassion that excludes nothing. Through radical compassion, you may feel a sense of social responsibility and a desire for the common good. Radical compassion can be an embodied experience where you feel a certain tenderness that extends to all beings. This feeling will move you to act out of a caring heart. Compassion is within every person, though some choose to cultivate this trait more than others. Those who don't choose to cultivate their compassion may find it being suppressed or overshadowed by cultural norms, social pressures, competition, jealousy, or criticism. To prevent this from happening, you must intentionally and consciously exercise your capacity for compassion. This is a more worthwhile endeavor than allowing your baser emotions to run free. While you may feel good hating others or criticizing others, this mindset takes a toll on you and will eventually have harmful effects on your physical and mental health. On the other hand, compassion can help you deal with distressing emotions (such as stress and depression) better and improve your sense of connection with others. These effects can improve your mental health and social relationships and enhance positive emotions.

That being said, it's not always easy to show compassion, especially to yourself. People may want to hold themselves accountable for their errors, and they mistakenly believe that self-compassion is wrong as it is too forgiving. However, compassion is not permissiveness or approval. You're not absolving yourself of all guilt and blame. If you treat yourself with compassion when you make a mistake, you're not telling yourself that the mistake is acceptable or no big deal. You're simply being more understanding toward yourself, telling yourself that everyone makes mistakes, and encouraging yourself to make amends and improve yourself. Another reason people don't want to show compassion to themselves is because they are often too hard on themselves and they see compassion as being too soft. This isn't the case at all. Often, people who are too hard on themselves express this through anger. They're often angry at themselves. Compassion can also be hard on you, but it expresses itself in a healthier way. Compassion can be firm, fierce, and strict, but it is never angry. So if you're hesitant to apply compassion to yourself for these reasons, put those misconceptions to rest. You only stand to gain once you start applying radical compassion to yourself.

Before you start learning about radical compassion exercises, let's study another component of this equation which is your inner voice. Your inner voice is made up of your past experiences that are all alive and active in your daily life, whether consciously or unconsciously. For people with healthy self-esteem, the messages of their inner voice are positive, understanding, compassionate, and reassuring. For people with low self-esteem, the messages of their inner voice are harsh, critical, punishing, and belittling. People with low self-esteem often have an overly critical inner voice that integrates a pattern of destructive thoughts aimed at themselves and others. They may become trapped in an internalized dialogue that leads to self-destructive and maladaptive habits. A critical inner voice will constantly work against you to lead you toward bad habits and discourage you from acting in your own best interest. This can severely impede your confidence, self-esteem, relationships, and performance. When your positive feelings are always undermined, and your negative feelings are always fostered, you will start to develop negative traits such as distrust, self-denial, addiction, isolation, and self-criticism which will all lower your quality of life. So it's all the more important that you combat your critical inner voice with radical compassion.

RADICAL COMPASSION EXERCISES

The first radical compassion exercise is called the Self-Compassion Break. This is a short and effective exercise that is easy to do. First, recall a situation or past event in your life that is causing you stress or pain. Think about this situation without judging it, simply think about how it makes you feel (emotionally, mentally, physically). Once you've gotten in touch with the feelings you associate with this situation, say these things to yourself: *This is a moment of suffering*; *I am hurting*; *This is stress*; *Suffering is a part of life*; or just *Ouch*! This will activate your mindfulness and you will be able to accept what you're feeling. These phrases can even help you recognize that suffering is something that all humans share in—pain and suffering are inescapable and unavoidable in life. This can offer you the comforting knowledge that you're not alone. You can supplement these phrases by putting your hands over your heart or performing whatever soothing self-touch is most effective for you. Other options for the phrase you repeat to yourself are: *Others also feel like this*; *I am not alone*; or *Everybody struggles in life*. You can even use phrases that are more specific to your situation, such as, *May I be kind to myself*; *May I forgive myself*; or *May I be patient*. This exercise can greatly relieve your pain as you are affirming your suffering and reminding yourself that it is a difficult but normal part of life. You are also committing to being kind, patient, or accepting of yourself.

The second self-compassion exercise involves writing. This is a three-part exercise that gives you the space to practice self-compassion. For the first part, think about the flaws and imperfections you perceive within yourself that you feel make you inadequate. Everyone has a few things that they don't like about themselves and that makes them feel unworthy. Consider the things that you feel insecure about. You can list as many as you want, or you can focus on one particular insecurity that is most relevant to you now. Notice how you feel when you think about these insecurities. Don't judge your emotions but simply allow yourself to experience them. As you learned through the previous exercise, negative feelings are unavoidable and an inherent part of life. And in this case, your negative emotions may even lead to positive results, such as self-compassion. So allow yourself to feel all your emotions and try to write about them. For the second part, write a letter to yourself from the perspective of an imaginary friend who loves you unconditionally. Writing from the perspective of an imaginary friend will allow you to extend to yourself the same compassion and understanding that you tend to show to your own friends. As you're writing from the perspective of an imaginary friend, try to create a persona of someone who is loving, kind, accepting, and compassionate. Then, imagine that they have all the same strengths, weaknesses, and insecurities as you. Remind yourself that this friend loves, accepts, and is kind to you. When you make a mistake or do something mean, this friend is quick to understand and forgive you. They also know all about your life, how you got to where you are, all the little choices you've ever made, and all the factors that have influenced the person you are today. With all this in mind, write a letter to yourself from the perspective of this imaginary and loving friend. The letter should focus on the insecurities and inadequacies you wrote about in the first part. What would this loving friend say to you? Would they expect perfection or would they accept your flaws? Would they understand how you feel? Would they judge you for feeling insecure or inadequate? Would they encourage you to accept yourself and remind you of your strengths? As you write this letter, make sure that this friend's love, compassion, and kindness shine through. In the third and last part of this exercise, you must put the letter you've written down and walk away for a while. Give yourself some time away from the letter. After some time, come back and read it again. Allow the words to sink in and imagine that this is really a letter from an unconditionally loving friend. Open your heart up to their compassion and allow it to soothe and comfort you. Try to imagine their compassion sinking into you and becoming your own compassion for yourself.

The next self-compassion exercise is aimed at changing your critical self-talk. This is an exercise that you must practice for a long time to fully reap its benefits. The first step is to notice when you're being self-critical. Notice what words, phrases, and tones you use with yourself. This will help you understand how you talk to yourself when you're being overly critical and negative. This can be practically and emotionally challenging so don't give up and keep practicing. The second step is to challenge your negative self-talk. Start responding to your critical inner voice. But don't take the same critical tone that it uses. Answering judgment with judgment won't be effective. Instead, use compassion. Tell your inner voice that you understand that it's nervous, anxious, afraid, or insecure, and explain that it's causing you unwarranted pain and distress. Ask your critical inner voice to allow your compassionate self to take charge for a while. This takes you to the third and final step. Reframe the observations and judgments made by the critical voice by placing them in a more positive and compassionate perspective. To do this, you can use the thought experiment of having an unconditionally compassionate friend. Imagine how your compassionate friend would view this situation and try to focus on the positive side of things. You can also supplement this positive self-talk with self-loving physical gestures. For example, give yourself a hug. This positive self-talk and physical gestures will encourage you to be kinder to yourself.

Another useful self-compassion exercise aims to identify what you really want and help you motivate yourself to achieve your goals in a healthy and effective way. The first part of this exercise strives to reduce the negative effects of your negative self-talk. Consider what you usually criticize yourself for and what you usually judge yourself as not being good enough at. Allow yourself to feel the pain of this criticism and offer yourself compassion for being judged and criticized. For the second part, challenge yourself to discover kinder and more caring ways to motivate yourself. Ask yourself how you would encourage and motivate a close friend or family member. Think about how a wise and nurturing role model would advise you on how your behavior isn't helping you reach your goals. Imagine what new ways they would recommend to you to help you move closer to your goals. Try to create the most supportive message you can think of that coincides with your underlying wish to be healthy, happy, and productive. For the third and last part, try to be more self-aware so that you can catch yourself whenever you're being overly critical and judgmental toward yourself. When you catch yourself being like this, just repeat the first part of this exercise. Allow yourself to feel whatever emotions are caused by your criticism, then offer yourself compassion for having experienced such harsh judgment. Once you've offered compassion to yourself, try to reframe your inner dialogue (repeating the second part of this exercise). Try to nurture your supportive, encouraging, compassionate voice rather than your critical and judgmental voice. This will bring about more positive changes in you as love is a much more powerful motivator than fear. In the next chapter, you will receive some extra quotes and exercises that can help you fully take advantage of the knowledge you've received so far.

Chapter Eight

POSITIVE PSYCHOLOGY EXERCISES, CBT WORKSHEETS, AND LIFE-CHANGING SELF-DOUBT QUOTES

In this last chapter, you will receive some parting supplementary material to facilitate your self-improvement. You will be led through some extra positive psychology exercises, CBT worksheets, and self-doubt quotes. These materials will help you take full advantage of this workbook, become better at self-appreciation, and offer you a fresh perspective on the errors of self-doubt.

POSITIVE PSYCHOLOGY EXERCISES

As you work on your self-esteem, you're bound to experience some positive changes, but you're also bound to face some relapses. No matter how much you work on yourself, every human remains susceptible and vulnerable to bad days and low moods. You may revert back to your old ways where you dislike yourself, doubt yourself, or overly criticize yourself. In such situations, you can try to use positive psychology to minimize the harm of such relapses and to put you back on the right track. To refresh your memory, positive psychology is a scientific method of studying human emotions, behavior, and thoughts that focuses on human strengths rather than human weaknesses, on building up the good in life rather than repairing the bad, and on upgrading an average life into a great life rather than only focusing on improving a bad life into normal, average life. These aims mean that positive psychology highlights the positive influences and occurrences in life, such as positive experiences, positive states and traits, and positive institutions.

One way to incorporate positive psychology into your everyday life is to use it to identify and ease your doubts. During a self-esteem relapse, your self-doubt may spike, and you may begin to doubt your worth, your progress, your skills, and everything else. You must learn how to realize when your self-talk has taken a turn for the worse. If you're self-aware enough, then it should be quite simple to realize that your tone, words, attitude, and phrases you use toward yourself have darkened. But if you're still struggling with self-awareness, simply try to raise a red flag to yourself whenever you hear yourself saying things like, *I can't*, or *What if?* Rather than thinking that you can't possibly do or achieve something, think to yourself that you can't do this thing for now but that you're working on it. And rather than thinking of all the negative outcomes that will happen if you fail, just tell yourself that even if you fail, nothing is stopping you from trying again. Changing your self-talk can transform a negative situation into a positive one where you have room for growth. This gives you the motivation to try and the grace to try again. Another form of positive psychology involves the halting of an action. That is, stop listening to people who bring only negativity to your life. Some people are certain that everything is impossible, they're quick to shoot down your ideas, and they're generally not hopeful about how anything will turn out. Being around such negative and unrealistically pessimistic people can poison you to become as hopeless as they are. So part of positive psychology is to cut out this source of negativity from your life. Don't allow others to steal your energy through their own lack of it. Instead, surround yourself with people who bring positivity to your life, people who are supportive and passionate, and people who inspire you and motivate you to be the best that you can be. These people are a healthy addition to your life as they can help lift you up when you feel down and lead you to see the bright side on your darkest days.

The next positive psychology exercise is to recall your successes. During a relapse, it can be hard to do this. Your self-esteem is down, you're not feeling very kind toward yourself, and you're doubting all your skills and achievements. In such a mind state, it can be much easier to remember all your mistakes and flaws. But this will only worsen your relapse, so you must try to do the opposite of your urges. So instead, recall all the good you've done. Try writing a list of all your successes, big or small. If you're drawing a blank, you can ask a close friend about what they think your achievements are. This can be a refreshing confidence boost. You may be able to acknowledge your achievements in the moment, but it helps to have a concrete, tangible list that proves that you've had successes and done well in the past. At the very least, this can assuage some of your self-doubts. Other than this, you must try to trust and love yourself. In a relapse, you often act as your own worst enemy. Try to overturn this and instead act as your own best friend. You deserve to treat yourself better. Conduct this thought experiment: Ask yourself what you would do if someone were treating your loved one the way you're treating yourself. How would you feel and act? Then ask yourself why you can't behave this way toward yourself. Finally, give yourself permission to try and to try again if you fail. Self-doubt will always crop up, you can never completely eradicate it. But you can get better at dealing with it. So every time it comes up, don't fear or resent it. Allow yourself to feel the doubt, accept it, and recognize that your doubts are only thoughts, they're not your future. And try, despite your doubts. And even if you fail, simply try again. Things won't always go perfectly, but if you never try, you'll always miss out on opportunities to improve your life.

CBT WORKSHEETS

The first CBT worksheet that you will receive is the Fact-Checking Worksheet. This worksheet can help you recognize that your thoughts aren't necessarily true. By working through this exercise, you will learn that thoughts are not facts. Sometimes it can be hard to accept that your thoughts are irrational or untrue, especially when you're overwhelmed by a certain emotion. But this worksheet can slowly guide you to that realization. This worksheet provides you with 15 statements and you must decide whether or not they represent a fact or an opinion. There is a correct answer for each statement. Through this simple exercise, you will see that you may have several emotionally charged thoughts, but that doesn't make them absolute truths. You must learn to differentiate between facts and opinions so that you can begin challenging your dysfunctional and maladaptive opinions about yourself and others. Below are the fifteen statements. Try to assign each one under the category of fact or opinion.

- I'm dumb.

- I'm unattractive.
- I failed the exam.
- I have no friends.
- Nobody likes me.
- I'm a selfish person.
- This will be a disaster.
- I will fail this test.
- I'm not good enough.
- I'm overweight.
- I am single.
- I will be single forever.
- My family is disappointed in me.
- I dislike my job.
- I'm not good at my job.

The answers for this worksheet are: opinion, opinion, fact, opinion, opinion, opinion, opinion, opinion, opinion, fact, fact, opinion, opinion, fact, opinion.

The next CBT worksheet is Cognitive Restructuring, and it uses the technique of Socratic questioning to help you challenge your irrational or illogical thoughts. The first step is to write down a specific thought—one you suspect is destructive or irrational, or one that you notice is bringing you a lot of distress and harm. Next, write down the facts that support and contradict this thought as a reality. What facts suggest that this thought is accurate? What facts call this thought into question? After identifying the evidence, make a judgment on this thought, claiming that it is either based on evidence or based on your opinion. Now, you will move onto the Socratic questioning phase where you will further challenge your thought. Feel free to rewrite your specific thought in light of what you've found by listing all the evidence down. These are the Socratic questions to ask yourself (and remember to write your answers down):

- Is this thought truly a black-and-white situation or does reality leave room for shades of gray? This question can help you determine whether you're using all-or-nothing thinking, making things unrealistically and unreasonably simple when they're in fact more complex.
- Could you be misinterpreting the evidence or making any unverified, baseless assumptions? This question opens you up to the possibility of personal error.
- Might others have different interpretations of this same situation? What might those interpretations be? This question persuades you to consider things from different perspectives.
- Are you looking at all the relevant evidence or just the evidence that supports the beliefs you already hold? This question encourages you to consider your personal biases and to be as objective as you can.
- Is this thought perhaps an overinflation of the truth? You may be basing your thought in some truth but then extending it past its logical boundaries.
- Are you entertaining this negative thought because the facts truly support it or out of habit? This question can increase your self-awareness.
- How did this thought come to you? Was it passed to you or learned from someone else? If so, is that person a reliable source of objective truth? This question helps you interrogate the source of the thought to determine if it came from a trustworthy source.

- How likely is the scenario of your thought? Is it the worst-case scenario? This question helps you discover how much you should realistically be worrying about your thoughts.

These Socratic questions can help you dive deep into the thoughts that harm and plague you, and encourage you to analyze and evaluate them.

Another CBT exercise to do is behavioral experiments. These are similar to the thought experiments you've done before only they put those thoughts into action. In thought experiments, you imagine a *What if?* scenario; in behavioral experiments, you test these *What if?* scenarios. One way to do this is to experiment with the outcomes that various thoughts will produce. For example, you can test the different outcomes that come from these opposing thoughts: *If I criticize myself, I will be more motivated to work*, versus *If I am kind to myself, I will be more motivated to work*. To test these two thoughts you would first try criticizing yourself when you need to work and record your consequent motivation levels. Then, the next time you need to work, you would try being kind to yourself and record the results. Finally, compare the results to see which thought was closer to the truth.

Moving on, there is also Pleasant Activity Scheduling. This is a useful exercise to do when you're having a bad day. Simply schedule some activities in your near future for you to look forward to. You can try to write down one activity per day that you will do over the next week. They can be simple or extravagant, as long as they're feasible and enjoyable. For example, watching a movie, having a good meal, or talking to a friend. It can be anything you enjoy (as long as it's not unhealthy). Other than pure enjoyment, you can schedule activities that give you a sense of accomplishment. This can have much longer-lasting and far-reaching effects. Overall, this exercise introduces some positivity into your life and helps you look on the bright side of things.

Speaking of the brighter side of things, another CBT exercise for you is to write self-statements that counteract your negative thoughts. In your battle to achieve healthy self-esteem, you may often be plagued by negative thoughts. To counteract these, try writing down a positive thought that directly opposes that thought. For example, if your inner voice keeps telling you that you're worthless, try writing down how you are a person of worth or that you are a person with potential. It will be difficult for you to accept these thoughts, but it's better than merely sitting with your negative thoughts. Over time, you will be able to believe in these positive statements more than the negative ones. A final CBT exercise is to visualize the best parts of your day. When you're feeling very negative, a good way to remind yourself of the good in the world is to remind yourself of the good you most recently experienced. So try to recall and visualize the best parts of your day. This can help you recognize the positives in your life.

SELF-DOUBT QUOTES

The final section of this chapter will offer you some great quotes on self-doubt to help you think of it and combat it in various ways. These quotes have been taken from multiple people and collected by Asad Meah (2018):

- Doubt is a pain too lonely to know that faith is his twin brother. —Khalil Gibran
- One of the ego's favorite paths of resistance is to fill you with doubt. —Ram Dass

- Love is strongest when we learn to trust in spite of the doubts. —Anonymous
- When in doubt, throw doubt out have a little faith. —E. A. Bucchianeri
- Your faith can move mountains and your doubt can create them. —Anonymous
- Doubt your doubts before you doubt your faith. —President Dieter F. Uchtdorf
- The worst enemy to creativity is self-doubt. —Sylvia Plath
- Uninstall self-doubt from your mind. —Anonymous
- The only limit to our realization of tomorrow will be our doubts of today. —Franklin D. Roosevelt
- When you doubt your power, you give power to your doubt. —Honore de Balzac
- Never let self-doubt hold you captive. —Roy Bennett
- Worry, doubt, fear, and despair are the enemies which slowly bring us down to the ground and turn us to dust before we die. —Anonymous
- The whole problem with the world is that fools and fanatics are always so certain of themselves but wiser people are so full of doubts. —Bertrand Russell
- Willpower is the key to success. Successful people strive no matter what they feel by applying their will to overcome apathy, doubt or fear. —Dan Millman
- If you are going to doubt anything in life, doubt your own limitations. —Dan Brule
- Doubt everything. Find your own light. —Buddha

- Successful people have fear, successful people have doubts, and successful people have worries. They just don't let these feelings stop them. —T. Harv Eker
- Doubts in your mind are a much greater roadblock to success than obstacles on the journey. —Orrin Woodward
- I've learned that the mastery of self-doubt is the key to success. —Will Smith
- In love, we often doubt what we most believe. —Francois de La Rochefoucauld
- I believe every day your life speaks to you—through experience, through the people you meet, and even through pain, fear, and self-doubt. —Oprah Winfrey
- I love it when people doubt me. It makes me work harder to prove them wrong. —Derek Jeter
- I must show no fear, no weakness, no doubt. —George R. R. Martin
- Removing doubt is like removing a blindfold. —Tim Fargo
- You have what it takes. Don't ever doubt yourself. —Anonymous

Hopefully, you can find inspiration to overcome your self-doubt and comfort to soothe your self-doubt from these quotes.

Taking Control of Your Own Life

※

You've officially reached the end of this workbook. Hopefully, you feel more empowered and prepared to improve your self-esteem. As you close this book and continue with your journey, I hope the information you've obtained so far can guide you along the way and fill you with hope and courage. And at any point of your journey, please feel free to return to this book to revise some theoretical information, look through the various exercises and worksheets, and read the inspirational quotes once more. To refresh your memories of everything you've learned and to solidify their place in your mind, here is a recap of all the topics you've gone through.

In Chapter 1, you learned about the fundamentals of self-esteem and explored two other concepts that relate to it: self-acceptance and self-love. You then studied how they all interlink and can affect each other. Though they're definitely not the same concepts, they can facilitate each other's growth. In Chapter 2, you learned about self-doubt and how it can be a thief of self-esteem. When you doubt your own abilities, accomplishments, and even worth, your self-perception will plummet and you won't trust yourself. This will harm not only your self-esteem but also your self-confidence. You then discovered the various causes for self-doubt so that you can better understand yourself and the possible factors contributing to your own self-doubt. In Chapter 3, you began to learn about treatment methods, specifically cognitive behavioral therapy (CBT). You realized how CBT can help you overcome your self-doubt. You were guided through the theory, function, and benefits of CBT, and were exposed to various CBT exercises aimed at increasing your self-esteem and self-confidence. In Chapter 4, you began learning about yet another treatment method that is positive psychology. You learned the definition, theory, and aims of this field of psychology. Then, you studied the concept of self-worth, which positive psychology aims to increase in you. Understanding both these concepts, you started exploring the positive psychology exercises meant to cultivate your self-worth. You even received several quotes on positive psychology.

In Chapter 5, perfectionism was addressed, since it is such a common thief of your self-esteem. First, you were led to understand the various facets of perfectionism: you were given signs that suggest someone is a perfectionist and an explanation of the three types of perfectionists. Then, you received exercises specifically tailored to reduce your perfectionist tendencies. In Chapter 6, another common thief of self-esteem was acknowledged, that is your past experiences and the possible shame you attach to your past. Shame is a destructive emotion that lies to you about your worth as a person. To overcome it, you explored what exactly shame is and how you should approach it. Then, with shame out of the way, you discovered how to explore your past to transform negative memories into positive ones. In Chapter 7, you learned about radical compassion and how it can help you cultivate healthy self-esteem. You received several radical compassion exercises to help you build a better life for yourself. In Chapter 8, you received supplementary material to the information you'd received so far in this workbook. Namely, you received more positive psychology exercises, CBT worksheets, and self-doubt quotes. You can use all this information to make your self-improvement journey more effective and efficient. Now that you have this recap of the contents of this book, your memory of all that you've learned should be more solidified in your mind.

As a last note, before you close this book, I want to say that working on your self-esteem is a daunting task, but it is a necessary one. Having low self-esteem or even inflated self-esteem can harm your life in countless ways. But once you develop a healthy self-perception and begin to like yourself more, you will notice how your life opens up and brightens day by day. And the only way to reap these benefits is to do exactly what you're doing right now: Making a decision to actively improve your self-esteem and taking control of your own life. So I hope the benefits you reap are many and joyous.

Thanks for reading my book!

I am grateful that, from all the books on Amazon, you chose my book. It is my hope that you found great value in it.

Before you leave, can I ask a small fraction of your time? I'd like to ask you to leave me a review on Amazon, or a star-rating; doing so is immensely helpful for an independent author like me.

This is one way you can help me reach more people, to spread the word how this book can potentially help others.

Scan to review:

Leave a review in US   Leave a review in UK   Leave a review in CA

$129 FREE

Achieve a Worry-Free Smile with these
12 Mental Health Books!

The Easy Way to Improve Mental Health

Therapy doesn't have to be so expensive and complicated. That's why we are giving you these 7 eBooks and 5 bonus workbooks so you can start improving your mental health right away, without leaving your home!

- **Stop Worrying All the Time**: Stop those nagging thoughts in their tracks with mindfulness and anti-anxiety tips expert CBT therapists use!
- **Do Therapy Your Way**: Start taking action with 5 BONUS workbooks, so you can start smiling, laughing, and enjoying life on your own!
- **Love Yourself, Love Others**: Enhance your career, relationships, hobbies, and more as you march through each day with confident self-esteem

Scan to download:

References

Ackerman, C. (2019, June 19). *What is Self-Esteem? A Psychologist Explains [2019 Update]*. PositivePsychology.com. https://positivepsychology.com/self-esteem/

Anthony, A. (2021). *What Principle Underlies Cognitive Behavioral Therapy*. Www.mindmypeelings.com. https://www.mindmypeelings.com/blog/cbt-principles?format=amp

Barthelmes, V. (2019). *7 Essential Self Esteem Therapy Worksheets | JV Flexibility*. JadoreVanessa. https://www.jadorevanessa.com/7-essential-self-esteem-therapy-worksheets/

Batchilder, R. (2021, April 3). *What is Self-Worth and How Do We Increase it? (Incl. 4 Worksheets)*. Rorybatchilder.com. https://rorybatchilder.com/what-is-self-worth-and-how-do-we-increase-it-incl-4-worksheets/

Cherry, K. (2021, July 20). *What Exactly Is Self-Esteem?* Verywell Mind. https://www.verywellmind.com/what-is-self-esteem-2795868

Economy, P. (2018, August 1). *17 Inspiring Quotes to Boost Your Self-Esteem and Self-Love Right Now*. Inc.com. https://www.inc.com/peter-economy/17-inspiring-quotes-to-boost-your-self-esteem-self-love-right-now.html

GoodTherapy. (2009, September 15). *Find a Family of Origin Therapist, Learn about Family of Origin Issues*. Goodtherapy.org. https://www.goodtherapy.org/learn-about-therapy/issues/family-of-origin-issues

Horne, C. (2020, November 23). *Defining Your Family Of Origin & How It Impacts You | Betterhelp*. Www.betterhelp.com. https://www.betterhelp.com/advice/family/defining-your-family-of-origin-how-it-impacts-you/

REFERENCES

Jangra, N. (2018). *What's the Connection Between Shame and Low Self-Esteem?* Welldoing. https://welldoing.org/article/whats-connection-between-shame-low-self-esteem

Lannette, J. (2019, March 27). *7 Magical Steps In Cognitive Behavioral Therapy, or CBT.* Thecounselingpalette. https://www.thecounselingpalette.com/post/7-magical-steps-in-cognitive-behavioral-therapy-or-cbt-change-your-thoughts-change-your-feelings

Meah, A. (2018, July 19). *35 Inspirational Quotes On Doubt | AwakenTheGreatnessWithin.* Awaken the Greatness Within. https://www.awakenthegreatnesswithin.com/35-inspirational-quotes-on-doubt/

Mind. (2019, January). *About self-esteem.* Mind.org.uk. https://www.mind.org.uk/information-support/types-of-mental-health-problems/self-esteem/about-self-esteem/

Morero, C. (2021, August 6). *Perfectionism Quotes - 39 Inspiring Quotes To Overcome Perfectionism.* SaturdayGift. https://www.saturdaygift.com/perfectionism-quotes/

Ochester, T. (2019, September 13). *Radical Compassion.* Midwest Alliance for Mindfulness. https://mindfulness-alliance.org/2019/09/13/radical-compassion/amp/

University of Alberta. (2020, August 13). Recalling memories from a third-person perspective changes how our brain processes them: Remembering your past as an observer affects your memories. ScienceDaily. Retrieved August 25, 2022 from www.sciencedaily.com/releases/2020/08/200813134553.htm

Made in the USA
Las Vegas, NV
08 July 2023